The Continuity of Christian Doctrine

The Walter and Mary Tuohy Lectures
John Carroll University

THE CONTINUITY OF CHRISTIAN DOCTRINE

by R.P.C. Hanson

with an introduction by Joseph F. Kelly

THE SEABURY PRESS • NEW YORK

1981
The Seabury Press
815 Second Avenue
New York, N.Y. 10017

Library of Congress Cataloging in Publication Data:

Hanson, R. P. C. (Richard Patrick Crosland), 1916–
    The continuity of Christian doctrine.

    Bibliography: p. 96
    1. Dogma, Development of. I. Title.
BT21.2.H36   230′.01   81-5299
ISBN 0-8164-0504-2   AACR2

This book is dedicated to Father Henry Birkenhauer, S.J.,
some time President of John Carroll University,
whose kindly and learned friendship was one of the chief
gifts conferred on me by that University when I taught
in it from January to May, 1979.

Contents

Introduction

In recent years biblical fundamentalism has been on the rise. With this return to the posture of *sola scriptura,* Scripture alone, the question again arises, as it has in other periods of Church history, of the Church's relation to the Bible. On the right, some Christians claim that all the Church can do is adhere strictly to the plain meaning of the biblical text and eschew any notion of development of doctrine or even of ministry, since development is merely a euphemism for abandoning rigid biblicism.

On the left, other Christians claim that the gap between the modern world and the world in which the Bible came into existence is so vast that modern Christians cannot truly understand the Bible and they are thus not bound by it. For these people, Christian doctrine or teaching is what modern Christians determine it to be, with no normative reference to the Bible or, for that matter, any earlier period of Christian history.

For most Christians, neither of these approaches is adequate. They recognize that the Bible was composed in a world far different from our own, and primitive biblical teaching cannot be transported unmodified into the twentieth century. The Christian Church must adapt its message to every age. On the other hand, these Christians do not wish to abandon the Bible. They want to be faithful to the biblical tradition and simultaneously responsive to the needs of the modern world. Is this possible? Can the doctrine of later generations preserve continuity with the Scriptures? Can the Church speak to the present and the future without ignoring the past?

These are serious questions and they demand answers. No one is better qualified to provide those than the author of this volume, the Right Reverend R. P. C. Hanson, Professor of Theology at the University of Manchester and Assistant Bishop of Manchester, Church of England.

John Carroll University has an endowed chair, the Walter and Mary Tuohy Chair of Interreligious Studies, the purpose of which is to bring to the campus prominent scholars to give classes and public lectures on topics of ecumenical interest. In the 1978–1979 academic year, the holder of the Tuohy Chair was Bishop Hanson, who taught and lectured on "The Continuity of Christian Doctrine." The classes live on in the memories of the students who took them; the public lectures, revised for publication, are reproduced here, having previously been given to an audience of faculty, students, and interested members of the general public in the Greater Cleveland area.

What makes this book particularly valuable is that for Bishop Hanson theology is more than a learned discipline. His learned credentials are, of course, superb. He has written books on the New Testament, the Early Church, Irish church history, and the situation of the Church in the modern world. He has edited patristic texts, translated them, edited collections of essays, and written several dozen articles. But he also brings a pastoral perspective to theology. He was a forthright and courageous bishop of Clogher, Northern Ireland, during a tumultuous period in that province's history. During his semester at John Carroll University, he was active in the pastoral affairs of the Episcopal Diocese of Ohio.

The Tuohy Chair aims to further ecumenism and does so by promoting ecumenical understanding. But understanding is not necessarily agreement. Bishop Hanson is a prelate of the Church of England, whereas John Carroll University stands in the Roman Catholic and Jesuit traditions, and university officials would not necessarily agree with all which the bishop has to say. On the other hand, Christians of every denomination can profit from his thoughts on this topic, and it is the university's hope that many will. This book well conveys Bishop Hanson's scholarship, but no writings can adequately convey the effect of his charming and vigorous personality on all who came in contact with him during his all too short stay in Cleveland.

John Carroll University Joseph F. Kelly
Cleveland, Ohio *Department of Religious Studies*

(1)

Are We Cut Off from the Past?

Continuity

At no point in the whole history of civilization has as intense and widespread a scrutiny of the past been made as today. At no point has skepticism about the possibility of our knowing the past been so emphatically expressed as today. Before we consider the question of the continuity of Christian doctrine we must first examine, however briefly, the question of whether any historical knowledge of the past, and especially of the remote past, is possible.

As historians have pushed their investigation of the past further and further, using new techniques and aiming at an ever more exact imaginative reconstruction, so they have become more conscious of the enormous difference of outlook which separates us from almost all past ages. Let me give a concrete example. If any of the audience had lived in Constantinople in the year 530 A.D. they might easily have heard one educated man saying the following sentence to another: *ho archimandrites ton akoimeton apologian poiei huper tou kephalaiou tou kai ek tou huiou.* This sentence has first to be translated out of ancient Greek for most people to understand it today. Translated it would run, "The archimandrite of the Sleepless defends the Filioque clause." But that does not tell us much. What is an archimandrite, and who are the Sleepless, and what is the Filioque clause? Well, we can duly learn that an archimandrite is the head of the ancient Greek monastery, that the Sleepless were an order of monks in Constantinople who maintained by relays a round-the-clock routine of worship, and that the Filioque clause is the expression "and the Son" added by many Western churchmen in the sixth century to the term in the original Creed of Nicaea and Constantinople applied to the Holy Spirit "who proceeds from the Father." But even after this explanation most moderns would be quite unaware of the significance of the defense of this clause by the archimandrite, of all the theological, ecclesiastical, and political consequences and nuances involved in this defense.

Above all, most modern readers would find it very difficult to envisage a society in which the opinion of the head of a monastery about an apparently abstruse and minor expression in a creed should be regarded as a matter of the greatest importance. How remote from us, how alien to us, seems such a situation! What chance could we have of understanding the minds of people in Constantinople in A.D. 530? They spoke a language quite different from ours. They lived in a pre-scientific age. Their ideas of the physical universe, of the origin of mankind, of the functioning of the human body, of the manner in which spiritual and divine agencies—if there are any—operate, of art, of history, of literature, of government, of psychology, of technology, were utterly different from ours. If we tried to reconstruct their total world-view we would have to abandon large parts of the enterprise through lack of evidence. A vast avalanche of events, of history, has fallen between us and them, permanently cutting off communication. And if this is true of situations as comparatively recent as the sixth century A.D. how much truer must it be of situations much earlier than that, in the first century A.D., in the second millenium B.C., and earlier than that at the beginnings of civilization in Sumeria and in Egypt! The mists of history quickly thicken and surely we must admit that for the greater part of its extent they are virtually impenetrable, even though we may deceive ourselves into thinking that we can occasionally and fleetingly penetrate them. How can we then have the presumption to imagine that it is possible seriously to reconstruct the minds and intentions of people who believed and wrote about Christian doctrine long, long ago?

Such are the arguments being widely canvassed among theologians, philosophers, and scholars today. To deal more concretely with a representative (certainly not an exhaustive) list of authors: we have to face the argument of men like Dennis Nineham, who in a recent book[1] denies any continuity at all to Christian doctrine, refuses to believe in the possibility of the past providing us with any viable norm for doctrine, does not believe in the survival of a fixed quantum of truth from the first century A.D. or in the possibility of finding an authoritative and consistent core of doctrine in the New Testament, sees little chance of the ideas of one culture surviving intact and comprehensible into the age of another culture, and seriously doubts whether the reliability of any historical account before about 1720 can be trusted. This is to revive, in a totally different form, the contention that Christianity has no essential connection with history, first put forward in an extreme form by Søren Kierkegaard and since adopted with various modifications by Paul Tillich and Rudolph Bultmann.

Another writer, much used by Nineham, is the eminent Cambridge historian J.H. Plumb whose book *The Death of the Past* conveys its own message in its title. For Professor Plumb the past is dead, though history is not. By "the past" he means "a created ideology with a purpose, designed to control individuals, or motivate societies, or inspire classes."[2] Until the advent of modern scientific historical investigation, all account of the past was apparently motivated ideologically, even the works of nineteenth-century historians such as Thomas Macaulay and John Motley and William Stubbs, though the eighteenth-century Edward Gibbon is exempted from this judgment whereas contemporary Marxist historians are not. The true purpose of history, which has only recently been discovered, is "to understand men both as individuals and in their social relationships in time," and this includes not only finding out what happened (which Plumb apparently thinks to be generally possible), but "why things were so and why they changed."[3] Further, the historian works with a purpose, "in the hope that a profounder knowledge, a profounder awareness will help to mold human attitudes and human actions."[4] And finally one principle or lesson can be derived from history "that the condition of mankind has improved, materially alas more than morally, but nevertheless both have improved," and this truth in its turn impresses on us the value of rationality.[5] Finally we can refer to the well-known work by the American scholar Van A. Harvey, *The Historian and the Believer*.[6] This is a powerful argument for the view that no conviction or belief can be proved from history, and that the Christian believer is positively handicapped in approaching the task of investigating history because his convictions are likely to disturb the delicate balance of historical judgment. I have no opportunity at this point of referring to the works of many other authors who have written in support of some of these arguments, e.g., of Maurice Wiles, of John Hick and the other authors of the famous or notorious book, *The Myth of God Incarnate,* nor of doing more than the scantiest justice to the arguments even of those authors whose views I have attempted to summarize.

II

It would be disingenuous of me to pretend that I agree with these arguments, for I would hardly have undertaken to write on the subject of the continuity of Christian doctrine if I thought that no such thing existed. Let me begin the process of countering them by referring to a subject which seems quite irrelevant. At Paestum on the western coast of Italy several miles south of Rome there have survived a number of ancient stone temples. They were built by Greek immigrants to Italy, perhaps in the fifth or fourth centuries B.C., much more than two thousand years ago. They did not arouse much comment until, during he last few decades of the eighteenth century, a number of British architects "discovered" them, as it were, and were greatly impressed by them. The influence of these temples can be distinctly discerned in some surviving examples of architecture in Britain, especially in the work of Sir John Soane. Here is an example of apparently dumb buildings—for there are no inscriptions on these temples—still retaining the capacity of exercising influence in a totally different situation and culture thousands of years after they were first built. Hans-Georg

Gadamer, in his magisterial work *Truth and Method,* has these words to say about buildings and statutes: "As long as they still fulfill their function, they are contemporaneous with every age."[7] Here is an example in which the remote past may be said to speak directly to each age in its surviving monuments. Every sensitive person must have experienced a similar communication when gazing at the Parthenon in Athens, the Hagia Sophia in Constantinople, at a great mediaeval cathedral in Europe, or even at the remains of the pre-Columbian civilizations in the continent of America. These monuments do not indeed give us an exact transcript of the psychological state of their creators, nor inform us much about the significance which those who built them attached to them. They do not tell us "exactly what happened." But, as we shall see, this is not the only criterion of historical effectiveness. It is enough for the moment to note that works of art such as we have been considering constitute an example of authentic communication in spite of the mists of history.

Let us now turn from ancient monuments to ancient historians. Dr. Nineham gives the impression that all ancient historical accounts are to be classed as equally unreliable from the point of view of the modern investigator. I think that he is here reproducing his own version of Professor Plumb's idea that all historians until very recently were so much obsessed by one ideology or another that, compared with the historian of today, they cannot be thought to be dealing with history proper but only with a more or less imaginary past. I do not for a moment believe that Plumb's distinction between the past and history will hold water or will be respected by future writers on the subject. It must at once occur to any intelligent reader of Professor Plumb's little work that, after dismissing almost all historians of previous ages as the victims of ideology, he himself betrays his own adherence to a very promising ideology. Why should any historian wish to advance the cause of humanity either morally or materially, and why should he value highly the exercise of rationality among historians or others? What does Professor Plumb mean by moral advance anyway? He would, I suspect, find it impossible to give a non-ideological answer to that question.

But let us return to the subject of the reliability of ancient historians. That very many annalists, chroniclers, and historians of antiquity and of the mediaeval period accepted legend and myth as true history and were to a greater or less degree uncritical in their use of sources, every student of history must admit. Anyone who, like myself, has had any acquaintance with mediaeval Irish hagiography will admit this more readily than most. But to use this general observation to condemn all ancient historiography as unreliable is itself a very uncritical procedure. When I was studying classics in Trinity College, Dublin, more than forty years ago, I was encouraged to think of the ancient Greek historian Herodotus as an untrustworthy source of information, one who too credulously took myth, legend, and hearsay to be equivalent to historical fact; but scholarly opinion has shifted, and I think rightly shifted, since then. Herodotus is now regarded as a good historian in his own right. An eminent American student of ancient history, Truesdell S. Brown, in his book *The Greek Historians*,[8] regards him as an historian as great as Thucydides, and describes him as "the embodiment of historical curiosity."[9] It was indeed this wide-ranging and versatile curiosity which apparently constituted the main motive for Herodotus in investigating history. Does this count, we may ask, as "ideology" in Plumb's sense of the word? It looks remarkably like the motive which, according to Plumb, impels most modern historians, i.e., "to understand men both as individuals and in their social relationships in time" and to find out not only what happened, but "why things were so and why they changed" (see above, p. 3). Indeed, by chance, Herodotus' accuracy has recently been remarkably vindicated in two separate instances. His description of the various ways in which the ancient Egyptians embalmed the dead has shown to be substantially true by modern research done on mummies.[10] And his account of the complete disappearance of an armed expedition sent by the Persian King Cambyses on a journey across the desert has been substantiated by the discovery of the remains of their bodies, arms, and equipment.[11] I may perhaps draw attention to another incident in Herodotus' *Histories*.[12] Darius, the successor of Cambyses, is campaigning in Scythia and has crossed the

Danube, leaving his allies from the Greek Ionian islands and coastal area to guard the bridge over the river while he attempts to find a route back to Persia round the Black Sea, whose size Darius had grossly underestimated. The Scythians evade Darius' army and reach the bridge before he can discover that his search is vain and return to the river. They invite the Greeks to break down the bridge and leave Darius and his army to inevitable destruction. Now, we might think that the Greek generals had at this point only two choices. Either they could refuse the Scythian request and remain honorably faithful to their promise to support Darius. Or, they could break down the bridge, return to their homeland, and encourage the movement of emancipation of the Greek Ionian cities from Persian rule, which breaking away was in fact destined to begin soon after. But Herodotus records that they did neither. Histiaeus of Miletus reminded the other leaders that they were all tyrants or despots in their native Greek principalities and that if the Persian power was impaired their chances of survival would be slight. So they decided to do no more than make a token destruction of the bridge in order to get rid of the Scythians. Darius and his army were saved. Not only is it likely that Herodotus was here relying on the work of an earlier historian, Hecataeus, who may actually have been present on this occasion, but the unprincipled realism of the Greek leaders' conduct has a ring of truth about it which we cannot miss.

I do not, of course, argue that Herodotus was as painstakingly accurate or as critical of his sources as a modern historian would be. I only maintain that it is very unwise to dismiss all ancient history as equally unreliable, or hold that we can see a common fault in all ancient chroniclers in the motives that impelled them to write and so conclude that it vitiates their historical judgment and puts them in a different class from modern historians. "Thucydides," says Truesdell S. Brown, "is often wrong, that was inevitable, but he thinks in historical terms."[13] One should perhaps note in addition that there were historical skeptics in the ancient world as in the modern. Pytheas, a famous mariner who lived in the last quarter of the fourth century B.C., was the first to bring to the learned world of ancient Greece the news that

Britain was an island to the far west. He claimed to have sailed round it. Some ancient historians believed him. But, others, Dicaearchus and Polybius among them, regarded him as a liar. They could estimate confidently the unreliability of ancient historical tradition and knew that Britain could not be an island.[14]

Again, the whole question of the possibility of people in one culture understanding people in a quite different culture is not as easily solved by a negative conclusion as Nineham thinks. Gerald Downing, in a penetrating review article devoted to Nineham's book,[15] has pointed out that it is an illusion to imagine that people absorb a single total culture and find themselves confronted by the totality of other cultures which are wholly alien to them. People live in a plural situation as far as cultures go, and are compelled constantly to switch from one to another and reconcile each with the others, and the first and second centuries A.D. in the Roman Empire offered as good an example of the existence of many cultures interpenetrating each other as one could wish. I may perhaps be allowed to illustrate this point by a more modern instance. I recently saw a good television program on the painter Rubens, the four hundredth anniversary of whose birth occurred in 1977. The commentator remarked that the outlook and background of Rubens differed completely from ours, and indeed seem alien to ours. And as we look at his elaborate mythological scenes representing people in violent motion, his historical tributes to the ruling classes of Italy, Spain, Flanders, and England, his large-bosomed, fleshy nudes, and the products of his rhetorical style, we can agree with this verdict. But the same commentator remarked that Rubens was also utterly different from his younger contemporary Rembrandt. Rembrandt, however, living in much the same age and society as Rubens, we regard as a supreme genius and we fully appreciate his introspective, quiet, melancholy art, full of depth and dimness. This does not at all support the view that distance in time inevitably means distance in sympathy, nor that any culture can be so homogeneous and self-consistent as necessarily to be wholly alien to us if any part of it is.

Again, there are undoubted instances of people in a later age being able to understand phenomena in the past better than an earlier age did. Two instances will suffice here. The book of Job we now acknowledge to be one of the profoundest, most important, and most moving documents in the Old Testament. We perceive that the author, though he never doubts the existence and sovereignty of God, discusses with astonishing freedom the problem posed by man's suffering and man's finitude, dismisses contemptuously conventional solutions to the problem and challenges God to vindicate his providence, and in the course of his dramatic exposition of the subject produces some of the finest poetry and most searching thought to be found in the Hebrew Scriptures. Almost all of this was lost on the Jews of the Rabbinic period and on the Christians of the early and mediaeval periods. To the author of the Epistle of James, Job was simply an example of patience (James 5:11), as he was to all the Patristic writers. Those who write commentaries on the book of Job, such as Didymus the Blind, the Arian Julian, and Gregory the Great, exhibit an almost complete misunderstanding of the purpose and character of the book. They sympathize with the conventional doctrines paraded by the author only to be condemned by him, and they tend to be rather shocked at the daring nature of Job's accusations against God and attempt to explain them away. They read a thousand other meanings into the book which are certainly not there, but they fail to see its main point. They seem to be wholly unaware of its literary splendor. Here undoubtedly the advancing years have brought a new and richer understanding of an ancient document. An increasing distance of centuries from its composition has brought increasing light. Cultures separated by twenty-one centuries have understood each other better than cultures separated by a mere six or seven hundred years.

The other example is provided by the anthropomorphisms of the Old Testament, those passages where God is represented in a human way, as baring his arm or changing his mind or sleeping or grieving, and so on. This troubled the Rabbis, but it gave much greater embarrassment to the Christian Fathers. The Greek philosophical thought in which they were steeped rejected such, as it seemed to them, all-too-human language about

God, and they took a great deal of trouble to explain it away. Most theologians of today, on the other hand, are not troubled by this at all, having an understanding of, and even admiration for the vivid, personalist language of Hebrew religion and piety in treating of God, and appreciating the advantage it has over the cold formal language of philosophy. Here once more antiquity, distance in time, has brought, not a fainter, gradually diminishing, but a greater and stronger insight and sympathy for the memorials of the remote past.

It has been suggested by several writers that the one basic factor which we have in common with the men of the past, whatever their age and culture, is that we share human nature with them. We can recognize them as human as we know ourselves to be human. This looks like an incontrovertible fact, but is has been denied or at least doubted by some, among them Dr. Nineham, who darkly hints that some sociologists are beginning to suggest that we have no right to assume, and no proper evidence for assuming, that there is such a thing as a recognizably common human nature in this case. The argument depends, of course, on what is meant by human nature. If we mean what the ancient Greek theologians meant by the word they used for it, *anthropotes,* that is an externally existent intellectual universal inadequately represented by particular instances of it who are called persons, then we may indeed cast doubt on the concept. But if we mean that it is possible that the men and women of, say, two or three thousand years ago who lived in Greece or Israel or China or Palestine may have belonged to a race or breed which was not human as we are human, but was subhuman or para-human, or that their psychological or nervous systems, their unconscious and conscious minds, were differently constituted or worked differently from ours, so that we have no right to argue from our reactions and feelings to theirs, this is indeed a very serious matter. If it means that they would not, for instance, be afraid of a charging tiger, love their children, wish to avoid economic destitution, be jealous of the success and popularity of others, desire to satisfy their physical appetites, and feel in certain circumstances moral obligation, then indeed we could not conduct any historical inquiry at all.

The investigation of history largely depends upon estimating the motives and intentions, the thoughts and desires, of people in the past. If we have no means of doing this because they were psychologically constituted quite differently from us, we cannot possibly reconstruct their actions, and past history becomes an indecipherable chaos. But much past history can be reconstructed; the known facts are very largely consistent with each other and fit into place, whether the historical investigation is being conducted by a Mexican, a Russian, or a New Yorker. It is inconceivable that all the attribution of motives, intentions, and desires to the people of the past are just bad guesses (though some of them may be), or are a phantasmagoria more like an opium dream than a genuine account of past events. To take this view would be to indulge quite gratuitously in despairing nihilism. The Stoic philosophers of the last two centuries B.C. and the first A.D. developed an elaborate, rational, and in some ways impressive account of human psychology, that is, the psychology of the men and women of two thousand years ago. It was based largely on empirical evidence. It can be to a large extent reconstructed. Modern scholars may not agree with this account of human psychology. But they can and do recognize it as a study of the same phenomenon as contemporary psychologists study—*homo sapiens.* The subject, though differently analyzed by the Stoics, manifestly displays much the same behavior as the subject does today. Indeed, this assumption underlies all study and appreciation of all culture, all art, the literature, philosophy, science, and religion of all ages. Skepticism about this principle is a skepticism which destroys itself.

III

Let us here turn aside for a short time to consider the relation of faith to history. It must first be realized that the truth of Christianity cannot be proved from historical data alone. It was the task of Kierkegaard to make this quite clear in an age which tended to be intoxicated with idealist philosophy. This philosophy claimed that, once history was viewed in the correct philosophical light, it could be demonstrated on historical grounds that Christianity was true, or at least as approximately true as any religion could be. Against this Kierkegaard declared passionately that apprehending the truth of Christianity involved the personal concern and commitment of the believer who believed the truth, and could not possibly be a matter of objective philosophical or scientific observation. He maintained that Christian faith needs no historical evidence at all, or only the barest minimum. In this conclusion he was followed for varying motives by both Tillich and Bultmann; they held that Christian faith is completely independent of history. Van Harvey, as we have seen, maintains that faith has no right to seek for proof in history. "No historical event, especially if assertions about it can elicit only a tentative assent, can as such be the basis for a religious confidence about the present."[16] We recall G.E. Lessing's famous dictum that "accidental truths of history can never become the proof of necessary truths of reason," which has recently been reexamined and to some extent reaffirmed in an essay by my colleague at Manchester University, Dr. David Pailin.[17]

In this chapter, I shall make only three points about this much debated subject. First, Kierkegaard was undoubtedly correct in maintaining that Christianity cannot be *proved* from historical (or philosophical or scientific) data alone. The truth of Christianity is known through making a decision, the decision and commitment of faith. This excludes the possibility of proof in a scientific, mathematical, or even perhaps a philosophical sense, because it is impossible for anyone to commit himself to something which is logically clear and true beyond contradiction, like a geometrical proposition or a demonstration that the earth goes round the sun and not vice versa. Van Harvey's argument will certainly hold against anyone trying to find proofs for Christianity in history. But that does not say very much, as the truth of Christianity is not discovered, and should never have been commended as discoverable, by that sort of proof. The second point, however, is that though faith does not operate with proofs, it does work according to *motives*. Nobody can have faith without having some motives for faith. If a housewife trusts a recommendation by a consumer magazine of a washing machine and buys it, her purchase is an act of faith in its reliability and the recommendation has awakened her faith.

Further, faith necessarily takes its character from the motives or reasons from which it springs. If I believe that the world is going to end in a fortnight because a passage in the Revelation of St. John the Divine says so, this kind of belief is different from the kind of belief that thinks the world is going to end because a nuclear war between two major powers has broken out. That history can and does provide motives or reasons for faith is so obvious that it scarcely needs arguing, even if we abandon the field of religious belief altogether. If a statesman pursues a foreign policy designed to secure the balance of power in Europe, he does so because his belief in the necessity of preserving this balance of power has been aroused by his consideration of what happened in the past when the balance of power was disturbed. Men and women join movements of protest, of rebellion, and take part in crusades for justice because of beliefs drawn from history. Nationalist movements rely largely on faith which is of a similar character. Half the participants and most of the propagandists in the English Civil War in the seventeenth century and the American Civil War of the nineteenth were similarly motivated by reasons drawn from history. Harvey in fact makes the admission—which seems to me a damaging one—that a fact can awaken faith or provide the symbol that faith can use.[18] If events in history can in these varied ways provide motives for faith in secular contexts, I cannot see why they cannot do so in religious contexts. There is nothing in religious faith which places its motives in a different class from those which supply secular faith.

Thirdly, both the sides of Lessing's famous dictum have recently been questioned. We have seen that the "accidental truths of history" (which incidentally is a very curious way of stating the subject) are not required by faith to become the *proof* of necessary truths of reason, nor anything else, because faith does not deal in proofs but in reasons for decision. And, on the other side, the concept of the necessary truths of reason, at least as far as truth as the object of religious belief is concerned, involves, as we shall see, an impossible attempt to emancipate the human mind from the historicality of its existence.[19]

IV

To deny that we can establish communication and at least a limited understanding with the men and women of the past, where we have any sufficient evidence of their existence and activity, is therefore unnecessary. Indeed, it is contradicted by evidence which should be plain to any person capable of understanding the methods of historical investigation. And whereas history cannot be asked to produce proofs of the truth of Christianity in the formal sense, it may legitimately be expected to supply motives for faith. Let us now move on to consider the subject of objectivity in writing history. This subject is brought forward by Harvey's objection that Christian belief upsets the delicate mechanism of historical judgment, and by Plumb's doctrine that all historians until very recently have been writing ideology and not history.

Van Harvey seems to me to have an exaggerated idea of the impartiality of historians. Indeed at times in his book he almost appears to write as if facts were small hard balls which historians have to find and arrange in patterns, and he seems to be quite unaware that knowledge of the past is affected by the knower. I am not, of course, arguing for complete historical relativism. This is a position which Nineham in his curious book at times seems to be nearing. It must be obvious to the meanest intelligence that if we are wholly bound by our cultural context, and can neither make generalizations about history nor enjoy any continuity of truth in history, then we cannot make the generalization that there are no universal truths surviving through history. But it can be stated with entire confidence that complete historical impartiality (which, incidentally, Plumb seems to think he has achieved) is impossible. Whether it would be desirable if it were capable of achievement I will consider shortly.

In fact by the nature of things no historian can be completely impartial. I will develop this idea first by an example. J.B. Bury was an eminent historian of the ancient world, one of the most eminent of his day, who first occupied a chair in Trinity College, Dublin, and later became Professor of Modern History at the University of Cambridge. He wrote a magisterial history of ancient Greece which is still useful. He edited Gibbon's *Decline and Fall* with notes. He wrote a number of weighty works on the Byzantine Empire. And then, in the year 1905, he published his *Life of St. Patrick*.

Scholarly work on Patrick had up to that point tended, as everything else in Ireland has tended, to run along denominational lines. Catholic scholars usually belonged to the maximizing school, accepting a great deal of later tradition about Patrick; Protestant scholars took the minimizing line, rejecting much of the later tradition. Bury was the son of an Irish rector, but had become a freethinker and agnostic. He was determined to show himself impartial, and in order to do so he came out on the maximizing, one might say the Catholic, side. His deserved reputation caused his views on Patrick to prevail for nearly fifty years. But now we can look back and realize that in his study of Patrick Bury made a number of errors which no historian of the ancient world ought to make. He spoke confidently about sources in a language—old Irish—which he did not know; he accepted as reliable very late and untrustworthy sources about Patrick, such as the *Annals of the Four Masters*, and he failed to notice a vitally important piece of evidence about Patrick, the quality of his Latin. His very desire for impartiality led him into grave historical blunders.

Harvey's warnings to the Christian historian are misplaced. They amount to a kind of psychological blackmail, and they should be rejected, as all blackmail should. Of course, the Christian believer must not allow his Christian beliefs to distort his view of historical evidence. But it is equally true that the non-believer must not allow his disbelief to distort his view of the facts either. One cannot deny, for instance, that Gibbon's dislike of Christianity distorted his view of some of the events of the early Roman empire. His unjustified reductions in calculating the numbers of Christians killed for their faith in the first three centuries is one example. His outrageous assertion that the

Arian controversy turned on a single iota is another. Harvey has no more right to warn the believer off the field of historical investigation than a Christian has to warn off a non-Christian.

The fact is that every historian uses as part of his technique in pursuing historical investigation a stock of general ideas, some of which he must have derived from other sources than his historical work, but some of which have been derived from or influenced by his study of history, and without these he would not be an historian nor find it possible to investigate history at all. He employs these ideas in making sense of the subject which he is studying, and they are inseparably bound up with the more exact and quasi-scientific techniques and judgments which have so much impressed Harvey. Harvey suggests that the orthodox believer brings faith to history.[20] But this is a false antithesis. Faith in the case of a believer represents something that in one form or another is part of an historian's activity. He can perhaps be a man without prejudices, but he cannot be a man without beliefs, and those beliefs will necessarily and rightly dispose him to make judgments not only about what should have happened or what could have happened, but about what did happen. His beliefs will even affect his attitude about "facts." This is not a matter of different historians giving different interpretations of commonly acknowledged "facts." It concerns whether facts are recognized as facts or not. Why do different historians estimate evidence differently, even to the point of whether facts are facts? Because they have different minds preoccupied with different collections of ideas, and there is nothing a priori to preclude Christian belief from being included in these ideas, and therefore conceivably influencing the historian's mind to recognize or not to recognize facts. The orthodox believer is not disqualified from writing history because he is an orthodox believer, any more than the non-believer is disqualified because he is a non-believer. Faith is not necessarily a state of mind alien to and inconsistent with the writing of history.

The whole subject of objectivity in writing history has been illuminated and placed in a new perspective by the weighty work of H.G. Gadamer already mentioned, *Truth and Method*. This scholar, who displays a range of learning which even a fellow-

German might envy, argues not only that complete impartiality in historical writing is impossible, but that it is undesirable. This apparently shocking thesis he advances with great cogency and persuasiveness in his work of 600 large pages. It has been the error of the human sciences too long to emulate the method of the natural or "exact" sciences. "The world of physics cannot seek to be the whole of what exists. For even a world formula that contained everything, so that the observer of the system would also be included in the latter's equations, would still assume the existence of a physicist who, as calculator, would not be an object calculated."[21] Further, the method used by the natural sciences excludes the possibility of history affecting it, what Gadamer calls "the historicality of experience,"[22] and yet this is an essential and inalienable part of historical investigation. Our own historical circumstances and the tradition which we inherit is a necessary part of our understanding of evidence from the past. We can never place ourselves, unencumbered by any presuppositions, exactly in the mental position of some person in the past, because we cannot know him without judging him by, or at least from, our own contemporary situation. A lengthy quotation will perhaps make this clearer:

> A person who imagines that he is free of prejudices, basing his knowledge on the objectivity of his procedures and denying that he is himself influenced by historical circumstances, experiences the power of the prejudices that unconsciously dominate him as a *vis a tergo*. A person who does not accept that he is dominated by prejudices will fail to see what is shown by their light . . . A person who reflects himself out of a living relationship to tradition destroys the true meaning of this tradition. Historical consciousness in seeking to understand tradition must not rely on the critical method with which it approaches its sources, as if this preserved it from mixing in its own judgments and prejudices. It must, in fact, take account of its own historicality. To stand within a tradition does not limit the freedom of knowledge, but makes it possible.[23]

As Gadamer puts it epigrammatically, all that the historian who searches for complete impartiality gains is to incur the prejudice of being free from prejudice. One of the main arguments of Van Harvey's book, if we accept Gadamer's argument, was cut away from under him five years before he published *The Historian and the Believer*.

As far as Christianity is concerned, it can be demonstrated with some ease that it stands or falls by historical continuity. I do not gather from Nineham's book in what sense he can continue to believe in Christianity once he has abandoned belief in the validity of its continuity. Presumably devotees of Christianity today claim to be in contact with some form of truth. Presumably they are not simply playing an enjoyable game or telling a pretty story or indulging in a comfortable form of self-delusion. Whether this truth is envisaged as consisting of communication with God, who must be true, or knowing the gospel, or even just finding a true paradigm or example, it must have some form. It cannot be completely formless nor wholly inexpressible. That form must have some relation to Jesus Christ, an historical personage, or at least a character believed to be historical. The form therefore must be related to the period in history when Jesus Christ appeared. Contemporary Christianity can only vindicate itself as authentic if it can show that it is related to this historical event. The subject of continuity cannot be evaded. Tillich and Bultmann misled us at this point. It may well be that contemporary Christianity has many other tasks and obstacles in order to authenticate itself. But this is a basic, preliminary, indispensable demand. Nineham denies that a fixed quantum of truth can have survived the centuries. This is a very curious and misleading way of referring to truth; it would be misleading even if it were applied to the development of scientific truth; truth cannot be weighed and measured. The question which has to be answered is, does contemporary Christianity encounter or reflect or express the same communication with God, or the same gospel, or the same paradigm or example as primitive Christianity did? Or has the process of transmission so altered the original that it can no longer be recognized? In this chapter I have attempted to clear away some of the immediate obstacles to answering this question. I have tried to make it clear that it is mistaken to discredit all ancient records; that it is possible for us to understand and reconstruct the past; that the type of objectivity demanded by Plumb and Van Harvey is not only impossible but positively misleading, that past situations and cultures are not necessarily forever alien to us, and that though we cannot prove the truth of Christianity from history, our faith can and does and should receive strength and encouragement from history. But the question of the development of Christian doctrine remains.

(2)
Newman and the Protestants:

Development

If we are to appreciate this subject we must first have some understanding of the status and function of Scripture, and for this purpose I wish first to deal with a Protestant misunderstanding. This misunderstanding is to think that Christianity consists of the Bible, that Christian doctrine is nothing more or less than large portions of the Bible, mainly the New Testament, transposed in a more or less unaltered fashion into articles or confessions or catechisms. If this were the case, then indeed we might find ourselves much embarrassed in trying to determine what is the authoritative core of doctrine in the New Testament, or the supremely important formulae, or propositions which must be regarded as unalterably true. Is it the Fourth Gospel or the Sermon on the Mount, or the Epistle to the Romans or that to the Hebrews, or all of them or parts of them? We might find it difficult to answer that question.

But in fact this is not the way to describe or define either Christian doctrine or Christianity. Christianity is the Church preaching the gospel of Christ, and Christian doctrine is what the Church preaches. But as soon as we say this, we must immediately add that at an early point in its career the Church bound itself by canonizing a number of documents which it called the New Testament; it set these, with the books of the Old Testament, for a norm of the Church's doctrine. It did so to prevent the erosion of its historical link with Jesus Christ by the waves of time, so that a collection of documents witnessing to the origins of Christianity should be a secure reminder of the shape and limits of its gospel. That this reminder and written norm takes the form of a number of different but not necessarily flatly contradictory interpretations of the significance of Jesus Christ is no bar to the New Testament performing its function. On the contrary, the very variety of the witness testifies to its primitive authenticity. The search for an authoritative "central core" of the New Testament is therefore misplaced.

Should we then, instead, describe the New Testament as no more than the starting point for doctrine? At times John Henry Newman, in his famous book *An Essay on the Development of Christian Doctrine,* writes as if all that the New Testament does is to serve as a basis, a soil from which the tree of development can grow, and no more. He appears to imagine that all that needs to be done in order to validate any doctrine is to show that somewhere, somehow, it has some basis in the New Testament, no matter how tenuous. But this is a serious mistake. The New Testament was not the beginning of Christian doctrine. As Irenaeus and Tertullian understood very well at the end of the second century A.D., the Church was preaching its doctrine long before a single page of the New Testament was written, and it continued teaching and preaching its message in uninterrupted continuity during the whole period of the canonization of the New Testament. The gospel is not bits of the New Testament transformed into sermons. It is the teaching of the Church according to the norm of the New Testament. The New Testament as an indispensable historical witness stands immovably between the Church of today and its origins. The old Anglican slogan "the Church to teach, the Bible to prove" puts the matter in its true light and delivers us from the necessity of detecting an authoritative core in the New Testament or distilling from it the essence of its teaching. It is impossible to separate the concept of the Church from the concept of the New Testament. Protestants who think that the two can be separated are under a delusion.

The New Testament is like a series of lenses through which the same object is successively viewed, or a drama in which different characters speak of the same person. It is a collection of evidence, and it is the business of the Church to determine the weight or burden or drift of that evidence, what Irenaeus called the *hypothesis,* and Tertullian the *ratio,* and Athanasius the *skopos.* If a jury listens to a body of evidence put before it, or historians consider the evidence for some important event in the past, they are not necessarily obliged to look for an authoritative core in the evidence, but to consider the effect of the whole. In short, if we abandon, as we must, the old idea that the Scriptures are inspired and inerrant, we can in place of these obsolete doctrines believe in their sufficiency and uniqueness.

II

"The Church to teach; the Bible to prove" is all very well, but what does the Church do with its teaching? What may it do? What has it done? We here face the subject of development, a preliminary survey of which will occupy us for the rest of this chapter. This is the problem of whether Christian doctrine has changed, and if it has why it has, and which changes are legitimate, if any are, and which not. The history of the study of development in doctrine has its origins in the Reformation, but it only reached conscious recognition in the eighteenth century, when Gibbon, Mosheim, Gottfried Arnold, Semler, and Münscher discovered and remarked upon the phenomenon of doctrinal change. The recognition was fully established in the nineteenth century with the work of Mohler, Baur, Newman, and Harnack.[1]

John Henry Newman, who must always represent to English-speaking theologians the most important voice on the subject of development, arrived at his conclusions independently of the work of Continental scholars, uninfluenced by contemporary German scholarship, either Protestant or Catholic, untouched even by any knowledge of a theory or theories concerning evolution. His classic work, *An Essay on the Development of Christian Doctrine,* published in 1845, was the result of his own reading of the Fathers, especially those of the fourth century, and his attempt, which was finally unsuccessful, to vindicate to himself the position of the Church of England and his membership in that Church. As is well known, in his book, published on the eve of his conversion to the Church of Rome, he boldly argued that development in doctrine had taken place, that the Church of Rome was the only Christian body which openly recognized this fact, and consequently that that Church was the only authorized Church, alone permitted to conduct and capable of conducting this development. Among other arguments he submitted the developments in doctrine achieved by the Church of Rome, and the life and behavior of that Church, to seven tests which, he maintained, it alone could successfully survive. Throughout his book he constantly pressed the question: granted that development took place in the dogmas articulated by the Church of the first five centuries, what reasons could non-Roman Catholic bodies produce for thinking that the development of doctrine had been arrested after the fifth century, and what machinery had they for dealing with development, and what criteria whereby to judge it?

It is not difficult to dispose of most of Newman's arguments in his book. They are mainly based on historical analogy, such as his comparison of the Church of England to that of the Donatists in the fourth and fifth centuries, and this is an uncertain and unconvincing method of argument. The reader is conscious throughout of Newman's capacity for special pleading. Much of the argument was effectively demolished by one of the ablest replies which it evoked, *The Theory of Development*, by J. K. Mozley.[2] First, Mozley singles out what must impress any reader of the book, the inescapable ambiguity about the meaning of development. Did Saint Peter and the other apostles know beforehand that the Son was consubstantial with the Father, but refrain from saying so publicly, or was this doctrine first achieved in the fourth century, and known, if at all, no more than implicitly by the apostles? Newman never seems to have made up his mind on this important subject. At times he seems to favor the first view,[3] at times the other.[4]

Mozley points out that Newman assumes without justification or proof that corruption in doctrine can only mean collapse or decay, and that no corruption could ever last long, and that therefore the Roman developments cannot be corruptions. "That is to say," is Mozley's comment, "so long as an idea goes onward at all, it is sure not to be wrong, the onwardness of the movement constituting its truth."[5] And later, "How 'power of assimilation,' 'early anticipation,' and 'chronic continuance' [three of Newman's tests of development] can prove a doctrine in a church, any more than a disposition in an individual, to be true, we do not see."[6] He points out that the example of the Eastern Orthodox Church contradicts Newman's assumption that the Roman Church is the only body to meet his tests of a true teaching Church.[7] Indeed, one of Newman's most curious traits is his assumption that he knows with confidence that all non-Roman bodies are doomed to speedy decline. All Calvinists, for instance, are in his view swiftly becoming Unitarians, all Lutherans "infidels." Mozley can also castigate Newman effectively for the curious idea that when the Fathers condemned a heresy as new they implied that in some sense the truth which the heresy perverted was also new.[8] And he has a good point when he maintains that it is wrong to speak of development of a doctrine in those cases where there is little or nothing to develop in the original revelation.[9]

But when Mozley comes to deal with the main point, and the main challenge, of Newman's book—the firm assertion that to say, for instance, that the Son is consubstantial with the Father is not precisely equivalent to what any of the gospels and epistles in the New Testament say about him, nor to what all of them say together—then Mozley's argument fails altogether. Newman, no matter how mildly and indirectly he hinted at the fact, did realize that the Christian doctrine of God has changed, that Justin Martyr and Irenaeus did not teach what Athanasius taught, and subsequent research has fully justified Newman's insight. Mozley not only does not solve Newman's problem; he does not even realize that it exists. He is still in the world of thought in which Bishop Bull in the seventeenth century answered Petavius and was admired by the Pope for having done so. He still can deny that any change or development had taken place at all, and apparently believes that the full doctrine of the divinity of the Son is directly revealed in the Scriptures, that the Apostles and the generations who immediately succeeded them believed in a doctrine of the Holy Trinity and in a Christology little different from that of Chalcedon.[10]

Nicholas Lash says justly that Newman's *Essay on Development* is "the fruit of a complex, personally acquired appreciation of the concrete facts of Christian history,"[11] and that we should realize the "fugal nature" of Newman's method of argument. He allows that Newman failed in trying to unite many different categories, logical, psychological, biological, and so on, in order to capture the truth of development; but still Lash says, "the impossible may, so far as 'the personal conquest of truth' is concerned, be sometimes more fruitful than the attainment of more modest gains."[12] It is also true that at times Newman's handling of historical arguments is such as to remind us forcibly that in the eighteenth century the study of history was held to be a department of the study of oratory. In reading Newman we are constantly struck both by his attachment to the past and his foreshadowing of the future. Further, there was a certain deviousness, perhaps unconscious, in Newman. He spent much of his life complaining that people misunderstood him, and it was not always their fault. One can even have a sneaking sympathy with the extroverted and unsubtle Charles Kingsley in the conflict between him and Newman which was (posterity has agreed) so clearly won by Newman. The controversy between them was rather like the encounter of a hippopotamus and an octopus. On this point of development, however, Newman looks like a man of the modern day, whereas Mozley seems not yet to have left the seventeenth century. The same can be said of George Salmon's book *The Infallibility of the Church* (1888). In destructive criticism of Newman's arguments in favor of the Roman Catholic Church, it is superb. In advancing a constructive alternative to Catholic doctrines of development, Newman's or any other, it is rudimentary.

If we could assume with Newman[13] that the Scriptures are no more than a starting point for subsequent doctrine and not a norm, then the subject of development would be much simpler. But all the early Fathers with unanimous consent held that the

Scriptures were more than a base; they were a norm. Doctrine, according to their view, had to be compared with the words of Scripture in order that it might be seen to be true. The Bible was a pattern, a criterion, by which doctrine was to be judged, and not merely the seedbed from which doctrinal trees should grow, the launching pad, so to speak, from which doctrinal space flights should take place. To accept this view of Scripture, which has every right to be called a Catholic dogma supported by the unanimous consent of the Fathers, is to render the subject of the development of doctrine a more intractable and complex one.

III

One point can be cleared up immediately. The impression given by Newman is that development inevitably takes the form of an ever-increasing mass of dogmas, logically or organically or even mystically related to each other in a vast and growing web. The best image for this concept of doctrine is perhaps the coral reef. The reef is created by the work of a multitudinous mass of little polyps toiling for ages at their task until finally the rock breaks the surface and becomes a reef and after that an island. The reef is the cumulatively produced body of dogmas, the polyps the theologians. In one passage Newman rejected the possibility that development could mean anything else than growth:

> The Mass and the Real Presence are parts of one: the veneration of Saints and their relics are parts of one; their intercessory power and the Purgatorial State and again the Mass and the State are correlative; Celibacy is the characteristic mark of Monachism and the Priesthood. You must accept the whole or reject the whole; reduction does but enfeeble and amputation mutilate.[14]

Newman cannot consider the possiblity of the development taking the form of a legitimate reduction, because his whole argument rests on his discovery that the doctrine of the Trinity achieved in the fourth century was a development, and that apparently the Roman Catholic Church alone was capable of accommodating itself to that truth. Development was in some sense a departure from or addition to Scripture and Protestants were unable to allow for such a thing, or, in the case of the Church of England, had allowed it but had refused to face this fact honestly. The possibility of the development as reduction, therefore, seemed to him irrelevant. As Nicholas Lash points out, between the First and Second Vatican Councils many theologians accepted uncritically the coral-reef theory of development, enlarging it in any irresponsible way, sometimes claiming Newman as their authority. The appeal which they regularly made to the judgment of the contemporary Church and to the devotion of the faithful against the witness of history brought these devout heirs of Pope Pius X nearer to the position held by the Modernists than they cared to think.[15]

But the possibility that development may take the form of reduction cannot be dismissed as easily as Newman dismissed it. There is no logical reason why the possibility should not be entertained. Even if it be granted that the doctrine of the Trinity and the Chalcedonian formula represents development, there is no a priori reason why development achieved at a much later stage in history should not legitimately take the form of a process of reduction or reformation. Newman was committed by circumstances to the conviction that, once granted that the Church of Rome is the only true Church, what it teaches must be right because the norm of right doctrine is that the Church of Rome teaches it.[16] But there is no universally recognized necessity to observe this principle. Catholic theologians have recently been endorsing the conclusion that the coral-reef theory of development is an unrealistic one. Nicholas Lash has asserted strongly that discontinuities and prunings-back must be taken into account as a serious possibility in development, and has condemned strongly the concept of what he calls "homogenous evolution" of dogma so popular between 1910 and 1950.[17] He quotes Schillebeeckx as coining the drastic phrase, "revelation through demolition,"[18] and Maurice Bévénot as proposing, as suitable examples of pruning in development, the abandonment of the doctrine of biblical inerrancy, of the condemnation of usury, and of the primacy of the Pope's secular jurisdiction.[19] And Lash insists that the mere accumulation of dogmas by the

Church does not in itself entail a greater grasp of the mystery which is at the heart of Christianity; that could only be so if all dogmas necessarily lead to more holiness.[20]

An important phenomenon, which has made the necessity of admitting as valid development which takes the form of reduction, is the progress since the time when Newman wrote his *Essay* of historical criticism of both the Bible and the history of Christian doctrine. This has compelled scholars of all traditions to face a radical reassessment of all Christian doctrines, has rendered untenable several of Newman's historical judgments, and has even begun to affect the Church of Newman's choice which, after declaring three new dogmas *de fide* within the span of one hundred years, has now as a result of the Second Vatican Council introduced into its life a freedom of scholarly research and thought which would have profoundly shocked Newman himself. The critical historical method has replaced the analogical. New means have been developed of distinguishing different intellectual and cultural sources and influences in history. We now can distinguish more accurately the Jewish and Hellenistic strains in early Christian thought, the Johannine and the Pauline traditions, the Gnostic, the Stoic, the Platonic elements. This kind of discipline inevitably tends towards an analytic rather than a synthetic view of the development of doctrine. Newman's test of "the power of assimilation" becomes suspect. The course of doctrine could at times quite reasonably be expected to concentrate on a distinction between what was assimilated and what original.

The Reformation in the sixteenth century was of course itself not so much a movement against the development of doctrine as an attempt at development by reduction, using the Bible as its criterion. It set off in each of the Reformed bodies a series of separate developments of doctrine, taking the form of Lutheran and Calvinist scholasticism and the appearance of an Anglican body of divinity. These natural and understandable tendencies were in the eighteenth and nineteenth centuries overtaken by the rise of historical criticism which has dominated all Protestant theological thought since. A curious result of the combination of Lutheranism and historical criticism has been a tendency in Lutheran theological circles to place ever earlier and earlier the point in the history of Christian thought at which reduction or reformation is deemed to be demanded, until now the point has been pushed back to divide even the New Testament itself.[21]

This movement of historical criticism is now beginning to dominate Catholic thought as well. Only the Orthodox refrain from it, "standing aloof in giant ignorance."

It would therefore be more in accordance with the facts to regard development of doctrine as a dialectical process, an affair in which both growth and reduction are involved, where both a gradual change in doctrine and a far-ranging reassessment of doctrine can legitimately be involved. In later lectures we shall see both phenomena taking place. We might compare development to a boat moored to a fixed buoy. It can float off in several different directions, one after another, at the bidding of wind or tide or current. But there is a point at which the cable attached to the buoy always checks its course, not always pulling it back to the same point, but always preventing it moving any further on its existing course. Or we could liken the development of dogma to a dance between the Church and Scripture;[22] the two partners are constantly in motion, sometimes moving in harmony, sometimes pulling against each other, but always inseparable. The image of a conversation or dialogue, which Lonergan has suggested as useful for understanding revelation and which has been endorsed by Lash,[23] might be a valid one, as long as we understand that it is a conversation which can never break off. Perhaps some of Henry James' novels give us the best analogy!

IV

The possibility of using Scripture as a norm for development has, of course, been rejected by several theologians, and in the course of this chapter I want to examine this subject rather more closely. In later chapters we shall look in much greater detail at some examples of development and then go on to consider more carefully the subject of models for development. It is a paradoxical fact that in recent years Protestant scholars have been in the van in denying the possibility of using Scripture as a norm, whereas Catholic scholars have paid far more attention than before to the task of controlling Catholic doctrine by the standard of Scripture. Maurice Wiles, in *The Remaking of Christian Doctrine*, has floated the suggestion that no norm of Christian doctrine is available, that we should perhaps regard Christian doctrine simply as a stream which wanders where it wills, that it consists in people reading and interpreting the Bible, people worshipping and preaching, with no discernible control and no check which is of any use to an intelligent mind.[24] We have seen earlier[25] that Dennis Nineham has argued that it is utterly impossible to detect any continuity in Christian doctrine or to use the Canon of the New Testament as a norm. Most recently David Pailin, in attempting to determine the standard by which Christianity can be interpreted, has rejected in quick succession the Vincentian Canon (*quod semper, quod ubique, quod ab omnibus creditum est*), Newman's seven tests, Karl Barth's concept of the self-authenticating power of the Word of God, the Bible and the creeds (on the grounds that they are open to a wide variety of interpretation), and the consensus of the Church (on the grounds that it is impossible to define which body of Christians represents the Church).[26]

On the other hand, Catholic scholars, representing a tradition which has recently enjoyed the experience of what might be called a return to the Bible, have shown themselves particularly sensitive about the relation of the Mariological dogmas of their Church to Scripture. Hans Küng, in his remarkable book *On Being a Christian* (E.T. London, 1978 of the German original 1974), gives a completely honest assessment of the biblical evidence about Mary and an account of Marian doctrine and cult up to the present day, remarking of the dogma of the Assumption, "There is nothing about this in Scripture or even in the tradition of the first five centuries. It appeared at first only in the apocryphal sources, in legends, pictures and feasts,"[27] and he approves of the marked loss of force experienced by the exaggerations of the Marian cult in the Catholic Church since the Second Vatican Council.[28] In his two essays on the development of dogma Karl Rahner handles the Marian dogmas very cautiously, admitting that the dogma of the Assumption appears (but only *appears*) at first sight to be totally devoid of any material upon which theologians can work,[29] and suggesting that it can be justified only on the principle of congruity (*convenientia*).[30] In his recent book *Foundations of the Christian Faith* (E.T. London, 1978), he gives just two pages out of 460 to the Mariological dogmas and those two pages are devoted to reducing the significance and blunting the novelty of these doctrines as far as possible.[31] In another direction Nicholas Lash, in his work *Change in Focus*, though he defends the Marian dogmas without attempting to minimize them,[32] is much concerned to establish that there is a continuity discernible in the history of doctrine. He suggests that it lies in "the unchanging reference of Christian doctrine to certain historical events; the pattern of the Church's liturgical worship; the fact that the Church has always been a structured community; and fourthly, that there has been a continuity of Christian meanings which was to be looked for, not so much in what has been said in the Church at different periods but rather in the concern or intention which has given rise to successive doctrinal statements."[33]

On this disputed question of a norm for Christian doctrine I confess that the Catholic scholars seem to me to have the right on their side. The arguments of David Pailin are not convincing. He suggests at the end of his essay that the proper way to find authenticity in the interpretation of Christianity is for the theologian to seek for a true understanding of ultimate reality, starting from the material found in the Christian religious tradition.[34] But what is the Christian tradition, or what criterion will the theologian use to determine the useful and valid parts of it? If he is to use the tradition he does so presumably because he thinks part of it, if not the whole, is true. He must therefore already have achieved some idea of a criterion or norm of truth in Christian doctrine before setting off on an authentication of the interpretation of Christianity, in which case is his journey really necessary? Again in dismissing the judgment of the Church as a criterion, along with the Scriptures, he has apparently failed to realize how inseparably bound up are the Bible and the Church, so much so that the whole concept of a Bible is meaningless without the concept of a Church. Unless we take the drastic course of abandoning the Bible altogether as an element in estimating the significance and truth of Christianity, we must recognize that the Church and the Church alone (however we define the Church) is authorized to interpret and capable of interpreting the Bible. The same paralysis of argument must overtake both Wiles and Nineham if they are serious in arguing, the one uncertainly, the other with an almost frenzied confidence, that there is no norm for Christian doctrine. Both of them in fact belie this argument by producing reasons for disliking and disowning a number of traditional Christian doctrines, such as the Incarnation and the Trinity and the Atonement. If doctrine can be repudiated, there must be some norm whereby that repudiation takes place.

The idea that the development of Christian doctrine should be reduced to *Religionsgeschichte*, to a story of activity without reference to criteria, to a picture of what one might coarsely describe as "one damn thing after another," is intolerable, and could only have occurred to someone who is dangerously divorced from serious Christian pastoral or theological concern. It is the reverse side, or, if that is thought preferable, the Protestant version, of that concept of uncontrolled dogmatic space flight which not long ago appeared to threaten the Roman Catholic Church and has now been decisively rejected. A Christianity without norms is a nihilistic Christianity, a Christianity of those who despair of Christianity. Dr. Nineham appears to have reached a position of almost unmodified skepticism. We are reminded of the tragic skepticism of the very late pagan poet Palladas:

> All is dust and all is a sick joke and all is nothingness, because the source of all existence is meaningless.[35]

It is difficult to believe that writers such as Wiles and Nineham, men of high education, distinguished abilities, and considerable learning, have really reached a position in which they are bound to regard the doctrine of the Assumption as possessing as much validity as the doctrine of justification by faith, or as little, and to assume that a fundamentalist interpretation of the Bible is no worse than one which takes account of historical criticism. But this is the logical consequence of abandoning in despair or satiety the quest for a norm for Christian doctrine. And if we are to find a norm of any sort we shall find it impossible to avoid referring to the Bible as constituting at least an important part of that norm. This is not all that can be said about the development of doctrine or the Bible as a norm. We shall have a closer look at several points already handled here, at criteria and models for development, for instance, when we have investigated in greater detail some moments of the process of development itself. But this must suffice for a preliminary survey of the subject.

(3)
What Happens When Christ Does Not Return

Examples of Development 1

I

One of the best ways of understanding the development of doctrine is, of course, to look carefully at the process as it takes place. In this chapter we shall examine one period in this process, and in the next another. Both periods are taken from the history of the early Church, both because this is an age in which I am less inexpert than in others and because the history of early Christian doctrine gives a picture of the Church encountering some perennial problems and attempting to find solutions to them for the first time.

The first development is the earliest and perhaps the most momentous, and at the same time the least appreciated of all. That is the development from eschatology to Christology. The fact that development in doctrine had taken place even within the gamut of the New Testament has been recognized only in relatively recent times. Neither Newman nor his opponents Mozley and Salmon were able to recognize this fact. Until general agreement had been reached on the order of composition of the Synoptic gospels, the date of the Fourth Gospel, and the pseudonymity of the Pastoral Epistles and the Petrine epistles, such a recognition was hardly possible. Again, until the eschatological nature of primitive Christian thought had been widely understood, such a recognition was most unlikely to occur.

Now, however, we can with some fair confidence reconstruct a picture of the development of early Christian thought in the first two centuries of our era. We must begin by putting the documents of the New Testament in their chronological order. The epistles of Paul are the earliest and, among them, the earliest is either Galatians or 1 Thessalonians and the latest probably Romans. Then comes the Gospel of Mark, then that of Luke and then Matthew's. We may regard Ephesians as a deutero-Pauline letter written not very long after Paul's death, leaving the position of Colossians uncertain. The date of Hebrews is a vexing problem; it might predate the Fall of Jerusalem, but if it does not it must not be placed very long after that event. We might regard Acts and Revelation as coming from about the same time, the reign of Domitian, though Acts might be dated a little earlier. The First Epistle of Peter might be placed at the end of the first century, and the Fourth Gospel about A.D. 100. We place the pseudo-Pauline Pastoral Letters early in the second century and with them the Catholic Epistles of John. Finally the Epistle of Jude and the Second Epistle of Peter, which are obviously related to each other, come latest of all, perhaps as late as the third decade of the second century. The Epistle of James is very difficult to date, but the indications are that it is late rather than early. Such are the findings of contemporary scholarship; the first book is not Matthew but Galatians and the last not Revelation, but 2 Peter. We can identify no work as coming direct from the hand of any one of the Twelve Apostles. These conclusions do not, of course, preclude our finding early traditions in books which are late, nor our drawing some conclusions about the life and thought of the Church at the earliest period of all.

At the latter part of this series we must observe the appearance of a number of works which are not in the Canon but which are contemporary with, and in some cases earlier than, the latest books of the New Testament, and whose witness is important as we trace the development of Christian thought. These are the *Didache*, parts of which have been by some attributed to a date as early as the Gospel of Matthew, if not earlier, the *First Epistle of Clement*, whose traditional date of A.D. 96 does not seem to me to be securely established and which might be dated later by twenty or thirty years, the *Letters* of Ignatius, the *Epistle of Polycarp*, the *Shepherd* of Hermas, the *Epistle of Barnabas* (about A.D. 125), and the *Second Epistle of Clement* (a mid-second-century sermon). We next can trace the fragmentary beginnings and strong development of Gnostic literature from about 130 onwards, the work of the Apologists, Aristides, Justin, Tatian, Theophilus, and Athenagoras, between 130 and 190, and, contemporary with the latter part of that period, the great work in five volumes of Irenaeus of Lugdunum, *Against the Heresies*. To these must be added a variety of mainly fragmentary Judaeo-Christian writings and apocryphal gospels and similar documents, such as the *Odes of Solomon* and the *Gospel according to the Hebrews* whose dates range from the late first to the late second century.

The reconstruction of the development of Christian thought from this literature is necessarily tentative and full of gaps, but it can be undertaken. It is clear that the most primitive Christian thought was dominated by eschatology. It is highly likely that the Resurrection appearances of Jesus were regarded by those who saw them and many of those who first heard of them as signs of the rapidly approaching End. The Messiah had risen and the general resurrection at the end of the world would follow shortly. It may be that traces of this belief can be found in Mark's gospel and that Luke's later gospel is intended, among other things, to discourage this belief. The thought of Paul is centered on the expectation of the Parousia, what we have come to call the Second Coming, in such a way that his doctrine cannot be fully appreciated until it is realized that he is writing for those who think themselves to be standing between the Cross and the End, in the overlap between the two Ages, this present evil Age and the Age to Come, the Age of the Messiah. Not only his theology but his ethics are deeply influenced by this conviction. The fact that the doctrine of the Holy Spirit appears unexpectedly in the Acts and Epistles of the New Testament, with very little preparation in the gospels (even in the Fourth Gospel), and constitutes one of the most familiar features of New Testament thought, is a testimony to the eschatological expectation of the primitive Church, for the Holy Spirit is an eschatological phenomenon, associated in late Jewish thought with the Age to Come, and his presence as a reality, not just a promise, means that the New Age in some sense has come. The Kingdom of God, proclaimed as near in the preaching of Jesus, has come. The "ends of the ages" have come upon the believers (1 Cor. 10:11); Christ has rescued them out of "this present evil age," into the New Age (Gal. 1:4) which represents a new creation (2 Cor. 5:17, 18) which is about to be revealed (Rom. 8:18, 19); the resurrection of Christ is the exemplar for the resurrection of all the faithful which is to be expected soon (1 Cor. 15).

Rather later, documents of the New Testament echo this expectation, though not so intensely. The Gospels of Mark and Matthew and the Epistle to the Hebrews are certainly looking forward to the Parousia, though not quite as confidently as did Paul. Luke-Acts has not abandoned this expectation, though its author may have realized that the Parousia had been postponed long enough to enable the gospel to penetrate further into the Roman Empire than the earliest Christians had expected. The First Epistle of Peter is full of strong though more tempered eschatological expectation, and the *Didache* echoes the primitive cry "Lord, come!" (Maranatha) of 1 Corinthians.[1] The Revelation of St. John employs a literary form which strikes us as bizarre and strange, but which was, we now know, very familiar both in the Jewish and Jewish-Christian world, the apocalypse. This book might indeed be called the highest peak in a submarine mountain range, it alone appearing above the water while the others have been drowned. But that it is an established literary form does not make it any the less an eschatological one; it presents us with an extraordinary mosaic or tapestry of eschatological motifs and images, and even though it speaks of an End that is arriving in elaborately designed stages, it still presents the Christian message in an entirely eschatological form. The same form is reproduced in several fragmentary Judaeo-Christian works, and even reappears in a reduced and domesticated form in Hermas' *Shepherd*.

Doctrine concerning Jesus, as a consequence, in its earliest form and in the greater part of the literature of the New Testament, remains characteristically Jewish and characteristically eschatological. In other words, it is dynamic, dramatic, and functional. Jesus is thought of much more in terms of what he does than in terms of what he is, and little or no attempt is made to relate his being to the being of God. He is called the Messiah, but the relationship of the Messiah to God in late ancient Judaism was by no means clearly defined and did not even necessarily imply divinity. In the early speeches in Acts, which may be the nearest clue in the New Testament which we possess to the Christological thought of the primitive Church, he is regarded as a man adopted by God to bring in the New Age; after his death he has been exalted to God's right hand, and he is soon to become the figure by whom the world will be judged. Even when in Paul and Hebrews we find a theology in which Jesus Christ is regarded as the continuation on earth of a preexistent divine being, he is still thought of in functional rather than metaphysical terms. Paul's profound and sometimes complex soteriology still tells us more about what Christ does than about what he is. The titles "Son" and "Lord" do not advance our understanding of Christ's status as much as has been thought in the past. It had been possible long before Paul's day to describe the Messiah as "Son of God" without implying any divine status for him. The identification of Christ with Adonai, God called by the Incommunicable Name, in several passages of the Old Testament, which is certainly an observable phenomenon in the New Testament, must not lead us to think that the writers were identifying Christ with God Almighty; this seems to me a wholly improbable opinion. They were developing their own peculiarly Jewish form of a doctrine of preexistence for the Messiah, reading his presence and activity back into their Scriptures and their sacred story. The rich stores of imagery and titles applied to Jesus in the New Testament, mostly taken from the Old Testament—Shepherd, Saviour, Pioneer, Amen, Stone, Temple, High Priest, King, Lamb, and dozens of others—are capable much more readily of describing Christ's function than of defining his relationship to God.

There are, of course, a few passages in the earlier literature of the New Testament which suggest a metaphysical or ontological relationship between Christ and God; Paul says that he "was originally in the form of God" (Phil. 2:6), that he is the "mind" of God (1 Cor. 2:16), and in the Epistle to the Colossians he is "the image of the invisible God, the firstborn of all creation, because in him all things were created . . . all has been created through him and for him, and he is before all things and all things hold together in him . . . who is Beginning . . . because in him all the fulness was pleased to dwell" (Col. 1:15–19). And the author of Hebrews can call him not only the Son, but "the heir of all things, through whom (God) made the ages, who is the radiance of the glory and impress of his substance, and who bears all things by the word of his power" (1:2,3). But in the first place these accounts of Christ are mostly only a preliminary to a description of what Christ did: he emptied himself, was obedient to death, and was rewarded with exaltation and the Name above all names; he reconciled us to God; he made purification for our sins. And in the second place, such passages as those which we have just reviewed are comparatively rare in the earlier literature of the New Testament. They are far outweighed by passages which give a dramatic and dynamic account of Jesus Christ. He comes down from heaven, he gives himself or delivers himself up, he makes purification or expiation, he obeys, he becomes a curse, though sinless he becomes sin, he removes the barrier, does away with the writing against us, offers himself to God as a sacrifice to end sacrifices, conquers, breaks the veil, brings in the kingdom and the New Age, frustrates the evil powers and breaks their sway, bears our sins, casts himself in faith on God, saves, reconciles, recreates, and so on. The terms used to describe him are typically Jewish; dynamic, not static; dramatic, not philosophical. He represents the Act of God, so much so that when he dies all die and when he rises all are offered the hope of rising. And all is envisaged within an eschatological framework (again a typically Jewish feature). All is presented within the pattern or picture of a Messiah or Saviour sent by God who was crucified, who rose again, and who is about to return in glory to wind up history (at a slower or faster pace) and judge the world.

II

Two pressures, however, combined to alter this situation. In the first place, the Parousia failed to materialize. The writings of the first decades of the second century, the Pastoral and Catholic

Epistles, the *First Epistle of Clement*, and the *Letters* of Ignatius, display a concern both for the details of Church organization and for the regulation of the lives of Christians living in a pagan society which are not evident either in Paul's letters or in the Book of Acts, and which are not consistent with an intense expectation of an early Parousia. Clearly as time goes on this expectation is fading. The matter is brought into the open by the Second Epistle of Peter, whose author attempts to answer the question, "Where is the promise of his Parousia?" His most unconvincing reply is that to God a thousand years are as a day and a day as a thousand years (3:3–9).

The other pressure arose from the fact that the Church by the beginning of the second century was moving out of a Jewish into a Gentile milieu. Christian teachers and evangelists were now increasingly meeting people to whom the Old Testament was unfamiliar and to whom the categories in which they were presenting the gospel, the Messiah of Jewish tradition who had died and risen again and was to be expected to arrive again in visible form on the clouds of heaven with angels, trumpets, and all the stage properties of apocalyptic literature, were strange and meaningless. The religious background of these people would be a diverse medley of pagan cults, and the intellectual background, if they were educated, would derive in one form or another from Greek philosophy.

These two pressures, the failure of the Parousia and the challenge of an un-Jewish background, must have constituted a considerable crisis for the Church. It could not behave like an ethnic group, such as the Jews constituted; it was committed to being a universal religion welcoming people of all sorts, all races, all backgrounds. Would it have been more logical at this point for the Church to dissolve itself, to admit that with the failure of the Parousia the bottom had dropped out of its religion and to recommend all its members to become Jewish proselytes treasuring the memory of the prophet Jesus of Nazareth? Should it have put all its energy into warning its people against that deadly corruption, the bane of German Lutheran theologians, Early Catholicism? Should it have fled at all costs the infection of a permanent official ministry, a body of metaphysical doctrine, an emphasis upon sacraments, and the rudimentary beginnings of a canon law?

In fact the Church did none of these things. It did not behave as if the bottom had dropped out of its religion. Perversely, it continued to draw large numbers of converts and to instruct them confidently in Christian doctrine. It met this crisis of doctrine by shifting the emphasis in doctrine from eschatology to Christology. The great document both witnessing to and effecting this change is, of course, the Fourth Gospel. The author of this document is very well aware of the various types of Christian interpretation of Jesus which have preceded him, Synoptic doctrine, Pauline doctrine, apocalyptic imagery. He is by no means a stranger to Jewish thought and speculation. He betrays considerable influence from contemporary Gnostic or near-Gnostic thought and terminology. And he fuses all these into a profound and brilliant interpretation of the significance of Jesus in which he deliberately switches the emphasis from the dreams of eschatological expectation to concentration upon the Person of Jesus. He is, here and now, the End, he is the Door, he is the Resurrection and the Life, all of which can be apprehended now by faith. C.H. Dodd has coined a splendid phrase for this, "sublimated eschatology." The author of the Fourth Gospel links this sublimated eschatology to the world of Greek philosophy by his preface in which he designates Jesus Christ by the word "Logos," a word which gathers up and harmonizes a number of different strands of thought, both Jewish and Greek, and declares that this Logos was with God at the beginning, and later became flesh. The perfect instrument had been forged for meeting the challenge which the Church had to face.

The Church did not use this instrument immediately. One of the most surprising facts about the Fourth Gospel, and one which constitutes the strongest of several arguments against its apostolic authorship, is that this document was not used in the mainstream of Christian life for about sixty years after it was written. It is not till we reach Irenaeus, somewhere between 170 and 180, that we can find an author who uses the Fourth Gospel confidently and frequently. We can find it used in circles remote from the mainstream of the Church. Basilides, the Alexandrian

Gnostic who flourished about 130, used it. Valentinus, the eminent Gnostic teacher who migrated from Alexandria to Rome, used it apparently in his *Gospel of Truth* about 145. Ptolemy, the highly intelligent Gnostic interpreter of the Jewish Law, used it in his *Letter to Flora* about 160. There are traces of its influence in various fragmentary apocryphal gospels. The Christ of the Gnostic gospels, such as the *Gospel of Thomas,* behaves like a parody of the Johannine Christ. Two relatively orthodox writers, writing perhaps just before Irenaeus wrote his *Against the Heresies,* Tatian in his *Oration* and Theophilus in his *Three Books to Autolycus,* quote the preface to the Fourth Gospel. Melito between 160 and 170 betrays a knowledge of it. But up to that point the silence is more significant than the allusions. We can find no definite trace of the work in the Catholic and Pastoral Epistles, Ignatius, Polycarp, Aristides, the *Epistle of Barnabas,* Hermas, I and II *Clement,* the *Didache* or Justin Martyr. It is not until Irenaeus champions the Gospel according to St. John that it enters the mainstream of Christian thought. He realized that if this was a Gnostic gospel it was a Gnostic gospel to end Gnostic gospels. Whatever its superficial appearance might suggest, its insistence upon the historical reality of Christ and its doctrine of the Incarnation were quite at variance with Gnostic assumptions and indeed rendered it a useful weapon against those Gnostic ideas which Irenaeus had set himself so strenuously to combat. He provided the Fourth Gospel with an historical pedigree guaranteeing its apostolic authorship which strikes modern scholars as too good to be true, insisted that there could be no more than four gospels, and brought the Fourth into the mainstream of Christian doctrine, where it has remained, immensely influential, ever since.

It is interesting to observe that even apart from the Fourth Gospel we can detect in the second century a tendency from eschatology to Christology accompanied by a use of Logos doctrine. Even if we put aside the surprising ascription to Jesus of the title "Logos of God" at Revelation 19:13, we can find Ignatius describing Christ by the enigmatic title "the Logos proceeding from silence,"[2] and we can discern in the *Apologies* of Aristides and of Justin, neither of whom can with confidence be regarded as indebted to the Fourth Gospel, nor even to Philo, something much more than a tentative use of a Logos doctrine. They attempt nothing less than a specifically Christian doctrine of God, in which, in the case of Justin at least, contemporary middle-Platonist philosophy is drawn in to create a theological system in which Christ is identified as a "second god," the immanent reason or Logos in God's being who becomes a separate but not independent entity for purposes of creation, revelation and redemption.

III

It is all the more important to spend some little time studying this development because precisely this development is, at the moment, under heavy attack from theologians of more than one tradition in both Britain and the United States of America. Van Harvey in his *The Historian and the Believer* appears anxious to reduce the central doctrines of Christianity to an atrophied form of justification by faith which leaves little room for a doctrine of incarnation. A book edited by John Hick called *The Myth of God Incarnate* carries a number of essays by British theologians rejecting or criticizing the doctrine of the Incarnation from several points of view. It is, as a piece of theological criticism, stimulating but incoherent. The essay by Frances Young can hardly be thought compatible with that by Dr. Goulder, indeed she virtually admits this herself. If Don Cupitt's desire to return to the Jesus of History, brushing aside the cobwebs of traditional dogma, is acceptable, than the argument of Dennis Nineham, that the historical evidence for the life and significance of Jesus is so much confused and so unreliable that no theories can be built upon it, cannot be maintained. I think it wholly unlikely that later scholarship will greet as a significant discovery the suggestion of Dr. Goulder that the doctrine of the Incarnation originated as an example of Samaritan Gnostic thought. The book as a whole must be regared more as a *ballon d'essai,* and a rather leaky balloon at that, then as a book which will stand as a landmark in the eyes of posterity, such as *Essays and Reviews* or *Honest to God.*

Much more formidable as an attack on the doctrine of the

Incarnation is the book produced in 1978 by G.W.H. Lampe, Regius Professor of Divinity in the University of Cambridge. This work is characterized by the solid scholarship which marks all Dr. Lampe's writing and presents a consistent and carefully thought out argument. Incidentally, some of his pages constitute excellent material for answering some of the objections raised in *The Myth of God Incarnate,* notably those of Dr. Nineham. Lampe's book is called *God as Spirit,* and it argues the case for a Christianity without revelation, without discontinuity, without eschatology: God has always been revealing himself to all peoples and cultures at all times. Jesus was a man under the guidance and inspiration of God, who is Spirit, to an exceptional and perhaps unique degree, but it would be going too far to describe him as God incarnate. He was not a Mediator. We have no need for a Mediator, because it has always been possible to experience and respond to the Spirit of God. Christians have always found and will always find Jesus an inspiring example and comfort and interpreter in their approach to God, but it was a mistake to weave round him a doctrine of incarnation and a greater mistake to develop further the doctrine of the Trinity.

Finally we might perhaps note that Maurice Wiles, Regius Professor of Divinity in the University of Oxford, has suggested in his *The Remaking of Christian Doctrine,* and in an essay in a book entitled *Christ, Faith and History* edited by Sykes and Clayton, both that it is wrong to imagine that God is closer to any one period of history than to any other, and that if we reject as unsatisfactory the classic formulation of the doctrine of the Incarnation, the Chalcedonian formula, we are logically bound to reject the Nicene Creed, for the two doctrines of the Incarnation and of the Trinity are bound together. We can therefore say with some confidence that the doctrine of the Incarnation, in spite of finding some eminent contemporary defenders such as Karl Rahner and Wolfhart Pannenberg, is under strong attack today.

We must, of course, allow that this doctrine is a development. Jesus did not travel around Galilee and Judea declaring that he was God incarnate. We cannot today believe that he was conscious of a continuity of existence with a preexistent Word, that in the back of his mind there was always a memory of his eternal life with God the Father as the Second Person of the Trinity. It is true that the Fourth Gospel, without giving us anything as developed as a doctrine of the Trinity, represents Jesus as conscious of a divine existence before his earthly one. But we cannot any longer take the account of Jesus in the Fourth Gospel as a piece of straightforward reporting of his actual words. This is not to say the whole gospel is a piece of sheer invention, but only to suggest that we must approach its text with a critical and cautious mind and be prepared to regard it as authoritative interpretation of the significance of Jesus more often than as an historically reliable source. But if Jesus did not declare himself to be God incarnate in the spirit and vocabulary of John's gospel, neither did he claim to be the Man from Heaven, the Second Adam, the life-giving Spirit and the Paschal Lamb as Paul described him, nor as the eternal High Priest and Pioneer of our salvation as the author of the Epistle to the Hebrews portrays him. However pleasant and simple it may have been for Christians during many centuries to imagine that Jesus gave us in his own words a relatively advanced and coherent interpretation of his own Person, this assumption is no longer possible for us today. We cannot fail to see in the New Testament's interpretation of Jesus Christ a history, a movement, a development. The Church has woven round the Jesus of history a growing tradition of interpretation, a history of doctrine. To shut our eyes to this fact is to court disaster and misunderstanding.

This certainly is development; it is the development of a doctrine of incarnation, whose materials can be found in other parts of the New Testament besides the gospel of John, but which only finds its actual realization in that gospel and in the literature of the second century. It is the development of a doctrine of the Person of Christ, and it is the beginning of a specifically Christian doctrine of God. Doctrinally it represents a most significant change from the early eschatological estimate of Jesus. But we cannot seriously describe it as wrong, distorted, unjustified, or unnecessary. The Church by no means abandoned its Jewish inheritance overnight, and eschatology, though to some extent pushed into the background, was by no means abolished. By this shift from eschatology to Christology certain inescapable needs were met. Jewish thought was not philosophical, discursive, speculative, but Greek thought was. Any educated intellectual of the Graeco-Roman world of the second century would want to know how the Christian related this Jesus who seemed to be the center of his religion to God, or to the divine, or to the highest reality. Existing Judaeo-Christian modes of thought were not adequate to answer this natural and unavoidable question. The shift from eschatology to Christology began to answer it. This shift did not represent a surrender to Greek or Gnostic thought. In a significant passage quoted by Origen, Celsus, the pagan intellectual who somewhere in the second half of the second century wrote a damaging book against Christianity from the point of view of Greek philosophy and pagan religion, objects that Christianity's doctrine of the Incarnation is *not* Greek. Jesus does not fit the Greek concept of an incarnate god because he lacks "grandeur, beauty, strength, voice, impressiveness and persuasiveness."[3] This passage is a serious obstacle for those who wish to derive the doctrine of the Incarnation from Greek sources.

It can hardly be denied that a doctrine of incarnation makes an essential appeal to history. God can hardly involve himself more compromisingly in history than in becoming human. And all through the ages the doctrine of the Incarnation has acted as a kind of stumbling block to the theologians and philosophers just because it seems to involve the Christian faith so irrevocably in history. Now, the involvement of truth with history is alien to the bent of ancient Greek thought. Greek philosophy in most of its forms tended to identify truth with permanence. The real was the unchanging. Supreme reality must be supremely immutable. But history is nothing but a series of changes, of developments, of events; it is a vast flux in which nothing ever remains the same. The notion that ultimate reality (that is, God) could become associated with history would have struck most of those who had been educated in Greek literature and philosophy as grotesque, if not an actual contradiction in terms. This fact weighs heavily against the theory that the doctrine of the Incarnation derives from Greek sources.

It must be remembered, too, what sort of a doctrine of incarnation ultimately become orthodoxy. Greeks, as Celsus suggests, might have tolerated a doctrine of divine epiphany, the story of a god who temporarily took on the form of a man to accomplish various purposes, and who during his period of human disguise manifests his godhead in various miraculous or sensational ways, as Dionysus does in Euripides' play *The Bacchae.* Or they might have accepted readily a doctrine of incarnation in which a man becomes god, and achieves deification or apotheosis because of his character or good deeds. Such a story was told about Herakles and several other figures of Greek legend and myth. But Christianity was driven by the nature of the evidence concerning Jesus to reject both these possibilities. I do not deny that some theological writing of some of the Fathers of the Church in the first few centuries appears to present the divinity of Christ in one or other of these two lights. There was, for instance, a persistent tendency in the orthodox tradition of Christology to underestimate, to fail to appreciate seriously, the real, the authentic, the irreducible humanity of Jesus. Clement of Alexandria, Origen, Athanasius, and Hilary of Poitiers are all at times guilty of writing of Jesus as of a divine being attempting to behave as if he were human and not always succeeding. But the final orthodox position, reproducing here the main emphasis of Christian teaching, firmly rejected this kind of interpretation. The evidence of the Synoptic Gospels could not be jettisoned. Jesus had suffered normal human weaknesses and limitations and finally the supreme weakness and limitation of death by crucifixion. The temptation to envisage Jesus as a man deified, raised to the level of a God, on the other hand, seldom attracted the Christians of antiquity. Somehow the iron law of Judaism that man is not God and can never be God had been deeply taken to heart. But this is a temptation which has enticed many theologians in the modern period. Lampe, for instance, at one point openly espouses this theory.

The fact is that the doctrine of the Incarnation is not one that lends itself to simple assimilation to ancient Greek models nor to quick solutions by facile modern theories. It was a complex, intractable doctrine which occupied the best minds in the

Church for most of four hundred years. On the one hand, the thought of the New Testament clearly was moving in that direction. The Prologue to the Fourth Gospel was no theological accident. It was a fulfillment of much Christian thought which had gone before. On the other hand, the evidence in the gospels pinned the doctrine of Incarnation down uncompromisingly to a particular, ascertainable character in history. The logic of these pressures was a slow and serious logic. It entailed movement in doctrine but not insignificant, capricious, or random movement. It would have been much easier for the Church to settle for a superficial, simple outcome for this doctrinal problem, one of several such available. But the Church would not take this course.

Again, by the middle of the second century the Church had inevitably begun to realize that it was an institution in society with a past behind it and a future before it. It could not continue indefinitely preaching a gospel within a framework of a return of Christ expected to be early, and absorbing intellectual and spiritual energy in that expectation. The movement to Christology relieved it of this embarrassment.

The Church was continuing to make converts, to attract minds of all sorts, to expand. There is no sign that its confidence was diminished or its sense of mission weakened by the failure of the Parousia to arrive. The shift from eschatology to Christology was not a sign of corruption, even though it paid the price of calling in the aid of Greek philosophy, at first unofficially and later explicitly. It was not a desertion of the Church's original message or mission. This shift was the presentation of the Church's message in another form necessitated by a different situation, and at the same time it was a discovery that the Lord of the Church was more significant than the framework of Jewish eschatological thought in which his message and word had originally been conveyed. Development does not necessarily mean distortion. It can mean discovery.

We should note that we have incidentally in this account rejected one example of reduction in doctrine. This is the contemporary form of the traditional Lutheran attempt to find the point at which doctrine ceased to be pure. Ever since

Lutheranism appeared in history, Lutheran scholars have pursued this cause. First the Magdeburg Centuriators, then Gottfried Arnold, then the men of the Enlightenment, then Adolf von Harnack, and in our day Käsemann and his disciples, have all attempted to set a point at which the faithful may begin to suspect the adulteration of doctrine and before which doctrine may be accepted as genuinely evangelical. And as each attempt is made the general tendency is to push the historical era at which doctrine begins to decay further and further back. With the Magdeburg Centuriators it was the sixth century. Sebastian Franck placed it at the death of the last apostle. Harnack saw signs of decline evident in the decision of the Synod of Antioch of 268. Rudolf Sohm detected it first in the *First Epistle of Clement,* about 96. Käsemann sees the rot beginning in the New Testament itself. "Early Catholicism" (*Frühkatholizismus*) can—alas!—be detected even there, so that we are called to create a canon within the canon.[4] Similarly, Van Harvey (a Lutheran) also can reject the idea that faith need be roused by the traditional doctrine of the Trinity, since it can just as easily be awoken by the demythologized picture of Jesus, a reduced paradigm of faith designed to encourage people to seek justification by faith, such as he presents in his book.[5] But the fact is that "Early Catholicism" was so early that it was there *in nuce* at the very beginning. "It is becoming increasingly evident," says Jaroslav Pelikan (another, but very different, Lutheran), "that this 'primitive catholicism,' with its movement from kerygma to dogma, was already far more explicitly at work in the first century than was once supposed."[6]

The unmistakable fact that the earliest Christian community, even at its most anarchic, charismatic, and uninstitutional, was quite confident that it had authority, and exercized that authority without hesitation in such important matters as the forgiving or retaining of sins, witnesses to the existence of potential Catholicism from the first moments of the Church's existence. Harvey is ready to conceive it possible that "the doctrine of the Trinity . . . is a way of preserving the formative significance of a past event for interpreting a present and living reality."[7] But if we ask how that "present and living reality" became present and living, we can only reply that it did so by the continuous existence and activity of the Church. In the first two centuries the Church under contemporary pressures, and for reasons which when examined appear reasonable and even compelling, canonized a body of documents which were called the New Testament, developed a permanent official ministry and began the process of compiling a body of official doctrine. To say that even before the New Testament was canonized the Church had gone too far in developing doctrine and was already compromising and unnecessarily complicating its message, and all this for the sake of reducing Christianity to the principle of justification by faith, is to be not only irresponsible but also unrealistic. When Marcion made a similar attempt in the middle of the second century he was irresponsible and unrealistic enough. To attempt this enterprise eighteen centuries later is to enter the realms of fantasy. We can agree with Pannenberg in describing the doctrine of the Incarnation as an irreplaceable development of the process of God's relevation and its climax in Jesus Christ, and "a final resumé of the God of Israel's history of revelation."[8]

(4)

Revolution in the Fourth Century:

Examples of Development 2

I

We turn now to the second example of development of doctrine which we are to examine, the development of the Catholic doctrine of the Trinity in the fourth century. Here we find a much more complex situation. It is more complex because there are far more sources available for the study of the subject, and because the dogma was developed as a result of a long and thorny controversy full of vicissitudes and much involved with non-theological factors, such as the intervention of the imperial government, the rivalry between the Eastern and Western Churches, confusion in the use of language, and inveterate local ecclesiastical feuds. It is also more complex because by this time the canon of the New Testament was virtually complete, whereas during the first two centuries it was only in the process of formation. Further, by the beginning of the Arian controversy there already existed a number of different and sometimes diverse theological traditions concerning the Christian doctrine of God which contributed to make the controversy more lasting and more stubborn.

Before we look at the example of doctrinal development which this century displays, I must say something about the Arian controversy in whose bosom this development took place. It is now nearly seventy years since the last book in English devoted solely to the subject of the Arian controversy was published. This is a testimony at once to the immense complexity of the subject, to the lack of interest in it to be observed among English-speaking students of theology, and also to the extraordinary unwillingness of English scholars to write books, a reluctance arising perhaps from modesty and perhaps from laziness. The consequence is that most students of theology whose only language is English have gained a quite unrealistic and indeed obsolete idea of the causes and nature of the controversy. The account of the controversy that is widely prevalent runs something like this: Early in the fourth century a wicked heretic called Arius started some highly unorthodox doctrine about the divinity of Christ. This dangerous heresy was soon answered, at the Council of Nicaea in the year 325, when the correct reply was given by the orthodox bishops, a reply which had always been available and which had for long been well known by all responsible theologians. But a small band of unorthodox, Arian bishops gained the ear of the emperor who succeeded Constantine and these were by their machinations able to overthrow the plans of the orthodox, prevent the obvious truth being openly acknowledged and prolong the controversy for another forty or fifty years, at the end of which period the villainous heretics were deposed, the suffering and virtuous orthodox reinstated and Catholic truth gloriously vindicated in the new version of the Nicene Creed.

This is a travesty of the truth. The only reason why this quite unrealistic picture has so long prevailed is because the last author to write books in English upon the subject—Gwatkin—unfortunately gave currency to this misrepresentation. Gwatkin branded Arianism as a thinly disguised form of pagan polytheism produced for the benefit of the pagans who were flooding into the Church, once it had been recognized and given approval by the Emperor Constantine. Gwatkin, who whatever his defects as a theologian was a good ecclesiastical historian, should have paused to consider chronology.

The Arian controversy began in the year 318 when Arius, a presbyter of the suburb of Baucalis in the city of Alexandria, fell out with his bishop, Alexander of Alexandria, on the question, how divine is Jesus Christ? At that time the Eastern Empire, including its most important city Alexandria, was governed not by Constantine, but by Licinius, a pagan who was prepared for reasons of state to tolerate Christianity but who had no interest in it at all. It was not for another six years that Constantine, then Emperor of the West, was destined to overthrow Licinius and become sole Roman Emperor, a contingency which nobody could then have confidently predicted. In 318 there was no incentive at all for pagans, anxious to scramble on the imperial bandwagon, to become Christians, and there is also no evidence that at that time pagans in the Eastern Empire were joining the Church in large numbers. Even if we ignore the other points on which Gwatkin's theory is vulnerable, we must reject it after a consideration of dates.

The idea that the Arian controversy was largely kept alive by plotting, politically minded Arians who could control imperial affairs needs to be revised also. The controversy as a whole is generally reckoned to have lasted at least sixty years, so that before half that period had elapsed all the original leaders on the Arian side were dead, including Arius who died, not much lamented, within ten years of the Council of Nicaea. Of course, we must allow that there were some depositions of anti-Arian bishops; when Arians could control imperial policy they did so.

But political moves following theological decisions were by no means confined to the Arian side. Constantine himself had set the pattern by exiling presbyters and bishops who refused to accept the verdict of the Council of Nicaea in 325 and shortly afterwards. Hilary of Poitiers in the year 364 made a determined effort to have the Arian bishop of Milan, Auxentius, exiled on a charge of heresy. He appealed, of course, to the secular power. Auxentius defended himself vigorously and Hilary's attempt failed, but it shows that if using political means to further theological causes was an Arian game, Hilary was ready to play the game.

Much more serious was the case of Athanasius, the great champion of orthodoxy, the resolute defender of the creed of Nicaea, the redoubtable enemy of Arianism. Because almost all our information comes from the side which won in the controversy, the side of Athanasius, he has been unduly represented as a virtuous and innocent sufferer, exiled five times on patently false charges, the victim of savage Arian contrivance. But two papyrus letters which turned up in Egypt about forty years ago have compelled scholars to change their opinion about Athanasius. They make it clear that he was no white-robed martyr, but a ruthless instigator of gang warfare and an employer of thugs. He was exiled always on charges of arbitrary and violent behavior, not on accusations of heresy. It now seems that there was considerable substance in those charges, even though the details of some of them could not be substantiated. The bishops of the Eastern Church displayed a settled dislike of Athanasius without ever declaring that he was a heretic. It appears that they had excellent non-theological reasons for their dislike. The later successors of Athanasius as bishops of Alexandria, Theophilus and Cyril and Dioscorus, were only following in the steps of their illustrious predecessor when they mingled Gestapo behavior with the intellectual finesse of a theologian.

The fact is that when the Arian controversy broke out nobody knew the correct answer to the question, "How divine is Jesus Christ?" There was no settled tradition of orthodoxy upon the subject; or rather, if there was such a tradition it was emphatically not embodied in the pronouncements of the Council of Nicaea of 325. Recent scholarship has not tended to vindicate Arius. I do not think that he can be vindicated. But it certainly has tended to domesticate him. He is not the extravagant horror from theological outer space which Gwatkin represented him to be. The exact origins and predecessors of Arius are a matter of intense scholarly debate conducted in at least five languages, and as each scholar undertakes to explain Arius he usually leaves a deeper darkness surrounding him than before; that is the way of scholarship. But at least the man is becoming more conceivable, more capable of being placed on an early fourth-century background. His views had enough in common with those of some of his contemporaries to prevent them being dismissed out of hand, but they were sufficiently unusual and bizarre to preclude them ever winning universal acceptance. He thus became the catalyst which precipitated a confused melée or theological stew which bubbled and boiled for a long time, and whose ingredients had been prepared over several centuries. In this controversy there came to a head a vitally important question which had been waiting for a satisfactory answer for a long time and had never received one. Once the question had been brought into the limelight by the action of Arius, it had then to be answered officially and definitely. But as nobody could produce a convincing answer the controversy lasted an exceptionally long time. The Council of Nicaea of 325 was of course an attempt to answer it, but it must be recognized that in this respect it failed. The wording of its formulas was ambiguous and open to misunderstanding. The Eastern bishops were entirely justified in regarding at least one of its statements as liable to lead to rank heresy, if not actually designed to lead there. It was, in fact, ignored by all the contestants in the controversy for more than twenty years after it had met.

I cannot possibly even outline the course of the Arian controversy in this chapter. All I can do is to call attention to the great development in doctrine to which it gave rise.

The first point to observe is that the development of the doctrine of the Trinity in the fourth century involved at least one direct contradiction of traditional, not to say Catholic, doctrine, and one reversal or reduction of a lively tradition of theological thought which had been entertained widely in the Church since the second century. The contradiction was constituted by the formal abandonment of an economic concept of the Trinity. There can be no doubt at all that the vast majority of the theologians of the Church before the time of Origen, and many after his time, had taught and believed that the Son was produced by the Father for the purpose of creating the world, revealing the Father and redeeming mankind in that created world. Some of them held that the Son had always been immanent in the Father from eternity, and for the purpose of creation was caused to become a distinct though not independent entity from the Father. But they certainly would all have said that there was a time, or possibly a situation, when the Son or Word was not that which he was when as the Father's agent he created the world. This applies not just to Justin and the other Apologists, but to Irenaeus, Tertullian, Hippolytus, Novatian, Lactantius, Arnobius, and Victorinus of Pettau.

Origen's concept of a graded Trinity in which the Son was

eternally begotten went beyond the doctrine of the economic Trinity and broke through it, but Origen's thought was unknown or without influence in the West until at earliest the middle of the fourth century. Now, the champions of the Nicene standpoint during the Arian controversy entirely denied an economic Trinity. This point is clear enough in Athanasius' frequent attacks upon the Arian doctrine (which had indeed plenty of support in the teaching of earlier ages) that "there was a time when he did not exist." It becomes crystal clear in the theology of the Cappadocian Fathers, Basil of Caesarea, Gregory of Nazianzus, and Gregory of Nyssa. So frequently do these fathers deny that there is the least interval, and particularly the least interval of time, between the Father and the Son, in spite of the fact that the Father generates the Son, that it is not worth giving specific references. Here is something which we must honestly call a direct contradiction between widely received earlier teaching that in its day ranked as orthodoxy and later orthodox dogma.

The reversal or reduction took place in the concept of the Logos doctrine. Ever since the time of the Apologists in the second century there had been a recurring tendency among Christian theologians to use the identification of Jesus Christ with the preexistent Logos as a convenient philosophical device. This was certainly not due to the influence of the Fourth Gospel; on the contrary those theologians, such as Irenaeus and Tertullian, who avoided this tendency, did so precisely because they could use the Fourth Gospel, and later the Fourth Gospel was to be Athanasius' chief weapon in killing this doctrine. But the temptation to give way to the influences of middle-Platonist philosophy and identify the Logos-Christ with the World-Soul or *Nous,* or some similar mediating reality, was too great for many theologians of the first three centuries. It gained much kudos for the Christian faith by demonstrating that Christianity could solve neatly a contemporary intellectual problem: how God or the Divine or the Absolute could communicate with the world, with transitoriness, change, becoming, while still being safeguarded from contact with it. Justin and most of his fellow Apologists had seized gladly upon this use of the Logos doctrine, and so had Hippolytus and Lactantius and Eusebius of Caesarea.

Above all, however, Origen had used the Logos doctrine for this purpose, building into his Trinity the Logos as second-grade god, by nature and constitution a mediator between the supreme, absolute God and the world. Eusebius was only reproducing Origen's doctrine, and when in one disastrous moment in his old age he declared that the Logos, since it was a mediator between God and man, could have been neither wholly God nor wholly man, he was sliding gently into an Arianism that had been prepared by Origen.[1]

Athanasius and Hilary of Poitiers, the defenders of pro-Nicene doctrine in the first half of the Arian controversy, directly refuse and deny this philosophical use of the Logos doctrine. To them the Logos was not there to safeguard God from contact with the world, but to guarantee God's contact with the world. The Cappadocian Fathers are even more explicit. They object to any doctrine which appears to make use of the Son for purely philosophical purposes, as if the Son was useful for achieving something which the Father could not do.[2] They go further and either reject or throw cold water upon the models and figures which earlier writers such as Justin and Tertullian had used to express the relation of the Son to the Father, as tending to subordinationism such as that of ray from sun, branch from root.[3] In short, the development of the doctrine of the Trinity stopped in its tracks with a firm "No Thoroughfare" notice, a theological development which might have been regarded as promising and creative, and certainly was so regarded by the Arians, and that because it made too many concessions to contemporary philosophy. This did not mean the end of a Logos theology, but it meant the end of that particular form of Logos theology.

It is worthwhile emphasizing these two points, first that the fourth-century development of the doctrine of the Trinity meant a contradiction of much traditional, indeed time-hallowed, doctrine, and second that in one respect it represented a reduction, perhaps even a reformation, of existing tradition, not in order to hellenize the Christian faith, but in order to avoid its hellenization in the direction of Greek philosophy.

Next, we must ask, what was the theological purpose of the

champions of the Nicene faith, of Athanasius and Hilary and the Cappadocians? Wiles in his *Making of Christian Doctrine* says that it was to safeguard salvation, which is clear enough but still vague; the Arians were anxious to safeguard salvation. He adds that the pro-Nicenes wished to ensure that salvation came from God and that the locus of salvation was man.[4] This is coming nearer the mark, because this was a program which Arianism could scarcely fulfill. But I think that this reversal of the Logos doctrine suggests a further and deeper purpose than this. They envisaged the Logos, not as a safeguard against God's coming too close to creation, but as a guarantee that he has come close to creation. They wanted to safeguard the self-communication of God, his self-giving, not, as they put it, in his *ousia,* but in his energy. This has always been the central scandal and test of the Christian faith. Is it possible to believe that God has really communicated himself in human form? Arianism could not accept this, neither the earlier tentative Arianism of Arius nor the later sophisticated, systematic, philosophically impeccable Arianism of Eunomius. This, I believe, is what the defenders of the Nicene faith were attempting to preserve both in the earlier and the later phase.

They were, it must certainly be admitted, greatly handicapped by their philosophical assumptions. They all formally subscribed to the philosophical axiom of the impassibility of God, which is certainly not an axiom honored in either the Old Testament or the New. Their attempt to meet the Arian argument that as Jesus Christ was manifestly vulnerable to suffering so the Son must have been vulnerable—doing so by taking refuge in a theory of two natures of which only the human one suffered—was unconvincing and was to make plenty of trouble for later Christological thought. But their philosophical presuppositions did not ruin their attempt to remain faithful to the original Christian tradition. Athanasius, as both Wiles and one of the latest and most convincing students of his thought, Meijering, admit, was not fundamentally interested in philosophy.[5] He used contemporary Platonic philosophy when it suited him but, as Meijering has shown,[6] he was quite prepared to repudiate it when he thought that it contradicted the truth of Christianity.

He was determined that the truth that in the Son we have the Father, that the Son is the revelation and communication of God and not his safeguard against contact with the world, should be accepted. His way of doing this was to insist upon the metaphysical stability of the Son, which he identified with his divinity. One might tentatively suggest that Athanasius meant by the metaphysical stability of the Son what the New Testament meant by his eschatological significance. He translated into the terms of his own day what he took to be the meaning of the terms in which the people of the first century had described Jesus. If he was not to use Biblical terms—and the history of the Arian controversy shows that it was futile in the circumstances to use Biblical terms—it is difficult to imagine what other means were open to him in order to safeguard what he took to be essential Christian truth.[7]

II

The case of the Cappadocian fathers is different. They were better versed in philosophy than Athanasius, and they used the terms of contemporary Platonic philosophy with much more confidence and deliberation. They were also maintaining a different argument, that is, the co-divinity and unity of all three Persons of the Trinity rather than the divinity of the Son alone, which was the main preoccupation of Athanasius. They have been accused of a philosophical confusion so drastic as to render their account of God as one *ousia* and three *hypostaseis* virtually worthless.[8] In order to affirm the authentic divinity of the three Persons they insist that each is *homoousios* and that their activities cannot be distinguished in our experience of them, and they therefore placed the distinctions, not in the data of revelation, but in the relation of the Persons to each other in the immanent eternal life of the Trinity, ingenerateness, generateness, procession, or however they be defined.[9] And they were reduced to "affirming a coequal Trinity, whose members stand to one another in relation of cause to effect."[10]

We must certainly acknowledge that in the thought of the

Cappadocian fathers we can see a clash between philosophical assumptions and fidelity to the Biblical witness. As Wiles points out effectively, Eunomius the Arian (their chief opponent in the field of Trinitarian theology) was a much more consistent philosopher.[11] His chief aim was to achieve a coherent philosophical picture of God: the Father was characterized by ingenerateness, the Son by an incompatible and inferior generateness and the Spirit by an even more inferior nature produced by the Son. All could be clearly and simply grasped by logical thought using the categories of contemporary Platonic philosophy. The Father by nature could not communicate himself, but he could quite readily be understood. The Cappadocians' thought moved in a different world, the world of the transcendent Jewish-Christian God who could never be fully understood and whose nature was such that men could only speak of it in stumbling and inadequate language. They are indeed constantly conscious of the inadequacy of human language, of the mystery of God's being, of the incapacity of the philosophical terms which they use to express either God's reality, or even their thought about God's reality.[12] This paradox of the coequal Trinity, whose members stand to each other in a relation of cause to effect, they are quite ready to acknowledge as a paradox. They do not present it as a neat philosophical solution to the problem of the Christian doctrine of God; they do not anticipate the lapidary glibness of the Athanasian Creed. But they were convinced that the full divinity of the three Persons must be defended while preserving the unity of the Godhead, and they knew of no other language in which to defend it. The Cappadocian fathers, says Pelikan, combined philosophical terminology with a refusal to go the whole way in speculative philosophy, and they admitted in the end that the distinction between what was common and what was distinct in the Trinity went "beyond speech and comprehension and therefore beyond either analysis or conceptualization." They fell back on saying that we must guard the tradition of the Fathers.[13]

But they also, in spite of their theological tentativeness and humility, insisted with a steady confidence that we can and do have saving knowledge of God, and that we know God in faith by his effects upon us, in other words at least partly by experience.[14] Now Trinitarian doctrine has always held, and rightly, that we do not experience the different Persons of the Trinity separately, in separate experiences. What we experience of God is God the Holy Spirit; the Holy Spirit could in one sense be described as God as we experience him (though not as our experience of God). The theological maxim *opera Trinitatis ab extra sunt indivisa* is that of a later day, but it is a sound and necessary one, and we cannot blame the Cappadocians for abiding by it. We do not directly experience God as Holy Trinity; the doctrine of the Trinity is a theologoumenon, not an immediate deliverance of faith. The reason why supporters of Trinitarian doctrine argue for a distinction of being within the Godhead is because they believe that this is the only way in which God's disclosure of himself in Jesus Christ can be guaranteed or understood as an authentic disclosure of Godhead. "The fascinating core of Christian theology is that God is as He reveals Himself, and that He reveals Himself as He is."[15] I do not think that the Cappadocians should be blamed for maintaining this doctrine, even though their having done so in the terms of late-Platonic philosophy involved them in some inconsistency. Wiles' drastic criticism of the Cappadocians can only be sustained on the doubtful assumption that the only evidence that is valid in arguing the point is the evidence of religious experience. This is surely a matter of distinguishing our experience of God and our understanding of him.

III

In summarizing this survey of the much more complex doctrinal development of the fourth century, we can perhaps observe that it was inevitable that the Christian faith should, in Pannenberg's phrase, be tested by an encounter with Greek philosophy.[16] The Fathers used philosophy freely, but they used it eclectically. Origen probably derived his concept of an eternal distinction of being within a graded Godhead from middle-Platonist philosophy. The pro-Nicene theologians of the next century accepted his concept of eternal distinction of being within the Godhead, but rejected a grading of the Godhead, and other examples of this discriminating use of philosophy could be cited, not all of them ultimately beneficial. Meijering's study of Athanasius is full of such examples. But we are not justified, as a consequence of this tendency, in regarding Harnack's famous description of the dogma of the Trinity as "in its conception and development a work of the Greek spirit on the soil of the Gospel,"[17] as a surrender to hellenization. In some ways their doctrine was a "dehellenization," and the hellenizing tendency was characteristic of "the speculations and heresies against [which] the dogma of the creeds and councils was directed."[18]

In a later work E.P. Meijering agrees with Harnack's definition of the process of making the early dogmas first quoted, but emphasizes that Harnack agreed that the Fathers worked "on the basis" of the Gospel. They did not desert that basis. In the process of working the data of the creeds into a rational and systematically grounded whole the Fathers indeed used Platonism as their tool, but they did not find it a tool ideally suited for their purposes. They were eclectic and by no means doctrinaire in their Platonism. In their enterprise of interpreting the Bible they did not directly contradict Platonism, but they did not swallow it uncritically. Meijering takes among other instances the great freedom with which Justin, Irenaeus, Clement, Origen, and Cyril interpret the apparently deeply Greek phrase applied to God, "beyond being" (*epekeina tēs ousias*).[19] Perhaps the greatest contrast of all is that noted by Pannenberg and approved by Meijering, that for the Jews God was completely independent of the rest of reality, and when he entered into relationship with it he did so because he chose to. For the Greeks, the ultimate reality was God, the highest conceivable form of what was there already, the highest stage of reality, sometimes so metaphysically remote and abstract as to be beyond speech and knowledge, but still conceivable, so to speak in a series, and in that sense bound to existence.[20] The Fathers never perhaps overcame this tension or contrast. But they did not compromise or betray it.

But we cannot doubt that a certain penalty was paid by this

development. Development always means closing some options as well as opening others. Certain possibilities were closed by the very use of the terms of Greek philosophy. It is significant, as has been pointed out more than once,[21] that Syriac-speaking Christianity arrived at a belief in the divinity of Jesus Christ without undergoing any philosophical development, but this possibility of a development in a different intellectual framework was overshadowed and perhaps ultimately caused to atrophy by the other. It would be interesting to consider whether a possiblity might or should arise of reopening the options closed by development.

Finally we must observe that a dialectic pattern, one which might legitimately be called a pattern of trial and error, has emerged in our survey of this particular fourth-century development. Indeed, the whole Arian controversy might be described as a prolonged process of trial and error. We shall have to take account of this process in the next chapter.

(5)

Will Anything Pass for Doctrine?

Criteria for Development

I

Before approaching the main subject of this chapter, I want to return for a moment to the topic of the continuity of doctrine. Catholics are apt to harp too much, perhaps, on continuity, but Protestants tend to forget it altogether. It is not a subject that can safely be forgotten. Protestantism, as Pelikan reminds us in his *Development of Christian Doctrine*,[1] has usually argued that the Church need not be continuous, but only faithful to Scripture. But Scripture would never have survived if the Church had not preserved it, copied it, printed it, circulated it, and taught it. No collection of documents alone creates or sustains a religion. We have today rediscovered the Dead Sea Scrolls, and we read and study them with interest and profit. But the religion to which they witness is dead because the community which produced, copied, and used these documents is dead. If Christians of any tradition enjoy a living faith today it is because that faith has been handed on, and the question of who handed it on and how, and what authority it has in being handed on, cannot be dismissed as unimportant. Pelikan puts this point in these words:

> At the beginning of his history Harnack speaks condescendingly of the tenacity of ancient dogma, and at the end of that history the theology of Luther is described as "the shattering of dogma,"

despite Luther's explicit Trinitarianism and almost Alexandrian christology. But if continuity is dismissed as tenacity, the true nature of the development of doctrine is inevitably distorted. For even in violent controversy and even in audacious speculation doctrine develops out of earlier doctrine within the context of the total life of the Church in the world ... Dramatic breaks and radical discontinuities are not all that is interesting about the process of development.[2]

If anyone wants to start a totally new Christianity, either from the Bible alone or from his own mind or his own experience, if anyone sets up a new church or a new sect, he rightly has to face the question, "What is your authority for this? What proof have you that your Christianity has any connection with authentic Christianity?," and authentic Christianity can only be original Christianity. If Christians today use sacraments and employ ministers, they have a right to be asked how they can be sure that their sacraments are authentic sacraments and their ministers' ministry is valid, how they know, in short, that God answers their prayers and confers authority on their ministers. The ingredients of continuity are well described in this sentence by Pelikan:

> The literature of the Bible, the forms of the liturgy, and the vocabulary of dogma have been a part of the equipment of the literate man of the West for so long that their atrophy threatens to make history unintelligible to the historian.[3]

And elsewhere he points out that even Protestants who see no value in structural continuity, continuity of ministry and sacraments and institutions, value continuity in doctrinal principles and in religious experience, and that Schleiermacher saw continuity in the experience of the Church, in "its memory, its witness, its celebration."[4] One suspects that many Christian bodies who think that they have cast off continuity are in fact existing unconsciously on the continuity of the Church before them.

This is the reason for the importance of the question of whether the continuity of development or reduction in doctrine (for reduction must also claim some continuity with the authentic past) is authentic or inauthentic, and why the question cannot be dismissed, as Wiles in his *Remaking of Christian Doctrine* almost dismisses it.[5] Manifestly, development will consist of both continuity and change. On the one hand, it is no longer possible to maintain, with Newman's early opponents, or with those who accepted before Newman's time a purely logical and not material development,[6] that nothing new has emerged, that the Church has in effect been merely repeating the doctrine of the Bible in different words since the second century, any more than it is possible to maintain that whatever new doctrines have emerged were well known to the men of the primitive Church, who did not happen either by design or accident to record them for posterity. This last was, approximately, Newman's attitude when he wrote his book *The Arians of the Fourth Century* in 1833. It is evident that even in the dogmatic formulations of the fourth and fifth centuries which most Protestants accept as valid something new was enunciated, perhaps one should say discovered. The discovery that the significance of Jesus Christ did not disappear with the fading of expectation of an early Parousia is a paradigm of other, later discoveries. These discoveries did not add to Christ, but in the course of reflection and experience and controversy Christians found more in Christ than their forefathers had found, or at least had consciously perceived. Pelikan has boldly suggested that the historical character of Christianity necessitates that in some sense Christian truth shall change: "The fact of change somehow belongs to the very definition of Christian truth."[7] Until recently, he argues, the assumption had been made that truth is unchanging and, with it, the divine or divinely instituted part of the Church. This view probably involved an assumption, explicit or implicit, that a relation existed between time and eternity, being and becoming, "by which history was assigned a lesser reality than the superhistorical realm, from which the truth of revelation was assumed to have come."[8] And Pelikan goes on to suggest that Christian doctrine includes metaphysical postulates and propositions, not in spite of the historical events but because of them. The Church must believe in the eternal preexistence and lordship of the Son of God as a corollary of what it believes of Jesus of Nazareth. Therefore "his historical immanence is no mere temporary episode in his cosmic and timeless career, but a constitutive fact about him," from which the doctrine of the Trinity can be deduced. The historically conditioned nature of doctrine is a kind of "presumptive evidence" that it has "been faithful to its character."[9]

On the other hand, development cannot simply be a completely uncontrolled doctrinal space flight, no longer moored to history, fueled by nothing except the vagaries of folk-religion or the whims of the Papacy. Nor can it be, the Protestant version of the same thing, simply an unrolling of *Religionsgeschichte*, an interesting historical phenomenon going its own way and nothing more, gripped by what Pelikan calls "the paralysis of a historicism that foreshortens the very meaning of dogma by treating it exclusively as a function of the time in which it arose."[10] Dogma is the dogma of a Church which "confesses about something that is true and ultimate."[11] Belief in dogma and acceptance of history are not contradictory but complementary:

> It is no less in accord with sound theology to insist that the Church's past be included as a full participant in this act of confession . . . Far from acting as a damper on theological creativity, this inclusion of the dead in the circle of doctrinal discussion acts as a stimulus to it . . . Relativism, by contrast, is hard pressed to show that dogmatic statements determined by a world view now past must still be taken seriously.

And Pelikan instances as examples of relativism Schleiermacher's statement that some doctrines can be "entrusted to history for safekeeping," and Troeltsch's consigning of much orthodox tradition to irrelevance.[12]

II

To these conclusions must be added an important qualification. When Newman wrote of development he apparently thought only of official or officially registered development, dogmas pronounced by councils or by popes without councils, not only the first four general councils of the Church (which the Anglican communion from which he emerged accepted) but the next three general councils, held in the East (about which the Anglican communion was undecided) and those many subsequent so-called general councils held in the West (which the Anglican communion decidedly rejected). In this spirit he accepted the two dogmas pronounced in his lifetime, that of the Immaculate Conception of the Blessed Virgin Mary pronounced by the pope unaccompanied by a council in 1854, and that of the Infallibility of the Pope pronounced by pope and council in 1870. But there is no obvious necessity that development should be pronounced or managed or registered solely by popes and/or councils. The history of general councils, after all, from the Council of Jerusalem described in the fifteenth chapter of Acts, through the Conciliar Movement of the fourteenth and fifteenth centuries to the First and Second Vatican Councils, does not constitute unequivocal proof that conciliar action is the best way of managing controversy, determining doctrine, or forming dogma.[13] There could well be other ways of doing this. The Reformation in the sixteenth century constituted a crisis of doctrine, and today we see signs that this crisis may be on the way to resolution. Hans Küng's work *Justification*,[14] in which apparently Barth accepts the doctrine of the Council of Trent, at least as interpreted by Küng, and the many agreements upon doctrinal points formally registered between Roman Catholics and Protestants,[15] certainly justify at least a tentative conclusion that such a resolution may be emerging. It may roughly be said to rest upon a realization by Catholics that the sovereignty of grace is an essential Christian doctrine and by Protestants that tradition is an indispensable ingredient in Christianity. This can reasonably be called development, though it has been registered by no ecumenical council, nor seems likely to be. And it can serve to remind us that development and reduction may be bound up together, as to some extent they were in the doctrinal development of the fourth century.

I do not agree with those who say that agreement on doctrinal matters such as that achieved by the commission representing the Roman Catholic and the Anglican communions is a mere papering over of the cracks, an agreement achieved by ignoring the most important issues and concentrating on the minor ones. A study both of the agreements on eucharistic doctrine reached by groups of Catholics in discussion with a series of different groups of Protestants in recent years and the publications of the Anglican/Roman Catholic commission suggests that a common method can be discerned in all. This method consists in ignoring the development of doctrine in the late Middle Ages and the period of Reformation and the Counter-Reformation, and returning to a consideration of doctrine in the biblical and patristic periods. The results are fruitful to an extraordinary degree, and will in the end, in my opinion, create a climate of opinion in which reunion will be almost unavoidable. This type of ecumenical discussion is, in short, solid, serious, and not to be lightly dismissed. It rests, of course, on the fact that all Protestants derive originally from a Western Latin tradition. Indeed, to an Eastern Orthodox, who does not derive from that tradition, a Baptist is not very much different from a Roman Catholic. This remarkable capacity for agreement also suggests that the policy of the reformers in the sixteenth century of returning to their roots, to the fountain of doctrine, in order to discover a means of renewal, was ultimately the right one, even though they may have carried it out in a somewhat rough-and-ready, amateurish manner.

For the enterprise of returning to our common origins in order to recover agreement and unity we are today much better equipped than were the reformers. We dispose of enormously more efficient tools for investigating history; we have a hugely greater capacity for putting events and movements in their proper perspective. There now exists, as there did not even as recently as fifty years ago, a scholars' International, a world of research and discussion and common encounter to be found in a multitude of books read by scholars of most of the nations of Europe and of the United States of America, of international periodicals and international conferences. This world is at once a sign and a means of cementing ecumenical understanding and a guarantee that this understanding will not dissolve into mere pleasantries or superficial formulae. The fact that I, an Anglican bishop, was invited to become Tuohy Professor at a Jesuit University and addressed its members in a public lecture is a striking proof of the existence of this world of ecumenical scholarship. We must acknowledge that today we live in a very fluid situation as far as doctrine and theology are concerned. It is a situation which must appear disturbing and chaotic to many, especially to those who have not been, so to speak, inoculated against chaos by receiving a training in historical criticism. But to compensate for this theological insecurity we can congratulate ourselves on the fact that the denominational barriers are down. We have come out of our sectarian fortresses and shaken hands with each other in No Man's Land. The war is over, except for pockets of fighting in the jungle, such as in Northern Ireland, where the news of the armistice has not yet reached them or where the firing is so intense that they cannot hear the message.

Indeed, the whole movement towards unity in contemporary Christianity, which is bearing fruit in these remarkable agreements across denominational boundaries which have been mentioned, can justly be seen as the proper logical result of a movement in the ecclesiastical history of the West which has been in motion since the end of the eighteenth century, whereby all the major Christian traditions have gradually been realizing at once their distinction from and independence of the State and the society in which they live and also the affinity which any Christian community has with any other in an increasingly post-Christian world. Another example of development might be seen in the history of the doctrine of the Atonement. Whatever view may be taken of the various forms which theories of the Atonement have evinced during the centuries, it can hardly be doubted that the Church has discovered more about the significance of the death of Christ than the Fathers of the early Church knew. With few exceptions they were not only not exponents of of the scandal of the Cross, they actively repudiated it. We can hardly doubt that subsequent ages, whether we look at late mediaeval devotion to the crucified Christ or to the atonement doctrine of John Calvin, understood more of this than did the theologians of the Patristic period.[16]

On a longer view, Luther's concept of sacrifice may offer an interesting example of the same process of the ultimate significance of Christian doctrine making itself evident, working itself to the surface, so to speak, after many centuries. Sacrifice was an accepted and uncriticized ingredient of almost all ancient religions, pagan, Jewish, and Christian. It is doubtful whether the Jews of the intertestamental period or earlier could have told us as accurately about what they thought sacrifice meant in itself as modern Old Testament scholars tell us, or think they they can tell us. Christianity accepted the concept of sacrifice unreflectingly because almost nobody could then conceive of religion without sacrifice. When Anselm's acute mind came to consider sacrifice at the end of the eleventh century it was no longer a concept which everybody took for granted. In his *Cur Deus Homo* he questions it radically and can only justify it by a kind of special pleading. In Luther's doctrine of sacrifice—as that which God gives to man, that is, the self-giving of Christ, not as something which man offers anxiously to God—the essential significance of Christianity has overcome and completely transformed this ancient concept and practice. We might consider here also the fact that the thought of Paul was not fully understood, not even by Augustine, until Luther realized its full implications. Here is an example of profound Christian doctrines waiting to be fully appreciated for fifteen centuries after they were written down. Christian truth may therefore take a long time to make itself evident.

III

But if we grant that development has taken place and that it is not all inadmissible, we must, before we go on to consider criteria for development, consider one apparently difficult question. Did not revelation cease, to use an old-fashioned term, with the death of the apostles? Or has revelation continued and does development represent a positive addition to revelation? Were the apostles in fact in the most impoverished situation, unenriched by the many revealed dogmas which have been poured out so richly upon the Church in the centuries intervening between the apostles and ourselves? This is a subject upon which

Newman, as so often, is ambiguous, and one upon which he was taxed by both Mozley and Salmon, in all the confidence of their ignorance of the development in doctrine (and perhaps in revelation) which their own church was committed to accepting. This apparent impasse is well handled by Karl Rahner in his two essays on the development of doctrine. Revelation is closed. We do not receive new revelations. But revelation is not a series of propositions, but "an historical dialogue between God and man, in which something *happens*, and in which the communication is related to the continuous 'happening' and enterprise of God."[17] The revelation is closed in that we can now only apprehend it through "the divine tidings and through faith which comes through hearing," not through any more immediate experience.[18] But though revelation is closed, this revelation is "the disclosure and openness for the absolute and unsurpassable self-communication of God to the created spirit." This means that revelation is dynamic and not like an inert object dug out of an ancient tomb.[19] The apostles apprehended revelation no less than we, but in a different way from those who were later to apply theological reflection to it in the light of later events:

> God allots to every age its mode of consciousness in faith. Any romantic desire of our own to return to the simplicity and unreflective density and fullness of the Apostolic consciousness in faith would only result in an historical atavism. We must possess this fullness in a different way.[20]

IV

When we turn, as we now must do, from establishing the inevitability of development to attempting to determine the criteria for development, we find that it is easy to draw up a list of criteria but very difficult to see how they apply. Scripture, tradition, and worship or religious experience are clearly the fundamental criteria which always have been applied and always should be applied. Or, as Pelikan puts it:

> To qualify as a dogma of the Church, then, a doctrine had to conform not only to the apostolic tradition, as set down in Scrip-

ture and in such magisterial witnesses as the decrees of the Council of Nicaea, but also to the worship and devotion of the Church Catholic.[21]

Newman, of course, suggested no less than seven tests of true development, but it is difficult to take them seriously today, so much are they argument not so much *ad hominem* as *ad ecclesiam*, and so far from impartial are the historical judgments upon which they are based. Wiles, in his *Making of Christian Doctrine*, recognizes of course the theoretical necessity of development submitting to the criteria listed by Pelikan, but, realizing how little it advances the subject to make this list, suggests two more useful criteria. "The determinative factor in ensuring the triumph of the new ideas," he writes, "was not so much their tidying up of the thought of the past as their creativeness in relation to the future."[22] Creativity should therefore be one criterion of development. Another criterion, he suggests, is what he calls "continuation of doctrinal aims," so that any development must be intended to be based on the record of Scripture, the activity of worship, and the experience of salvation.[23] But in his later work, *The Remaking of Christian Doctrine*, he declares that there can be no legitimacy or illegitimacy of doctrinal development but only certain continuing activities, expounding Scripture, worship, the experience of salvation. These, he thinks, do not constitute norms.[24] How it is possible to expound Scripture without either making or observing norms he does not, in the course of a short work, sufficiently explain.

Perhaps instead of drawing up abstract principles we might discover something more about the criteria for doctrinal development by taking a concrete and controversial example. So we shall now turn to consider in the light of our survey of the subject of the continuity of doctrine the dogma of the corporeal assumption into heaven of the Blessed Virgin Mary.

We have already seen in the first chapter how flimsy and sparse, on the admission of Rahner himself, are the antecedents in history and in tradition for this development. The only possible passage in the Bible to which appeal might be made is the picture of the woman seen in heaven, clothed with the sun and with the moon under her feet, about to give birth to a child, in the fourteenth chapter of Revelation. This is not a promising passage, because the woman is to give birth to the child after apparently leaving heaven and spending some time in the wilderness. As support for a dogma of the eternal preexistence of Mary it might be a promising passage, but not for her assumption into heaven. The movement is in the wrong direction. If any clear meaning can be assigned to it, the passage should perhaps be referred to the Church, who appears as a woman in the second-century apocalypse called the *Shepherd* of Hermas. Certainly no church father for the first four hundred years interprets this passage as referring to Mary's assumption into heaven. But then no authority of any sort whatever makes any reference to this dogma until about the year 400. And then the few authorities who refer to it are of a Gnostic cast and rather suspect, and it is many hundreds of years after that before the doctrine becomes anything like a theological commonplace. It is difficult to know if the dogma is supposed to have any connection at all with history; one would suppose that a corporeal assumption would necessarily demand some historical evidence before it could be believed. But this event—if event it be—is totally devoid of any historical evidence that could endure a moment's scrutiny.

Does this dogma, then, as Rahner suggests, rest wholly upon theological suitability and congruity and on the fact that it is universally believed in the Roman Catholic Church? If it is supposed in any sense to be an historical event, theological congruity will not help at all here. A thousand million people stretching over a millennium might believe in an event thinking it highly congruous, but if there was no evidence for it this would not add in the slightest to the proof that it had happened. Supposing, however, we say that this dogma has nothing seriously to do with history, that it is a theological judgment, a pious conviction based purely on theological congruity, a kind of development or extension of the dogma of the Immaculate Conception, what then? Well, clearly we must pause to consider briefly the influence of piety on doctrine, a subject which is long overdue in the course of this discussion.

There can be no doubt that piety has affected doctrine. Wiles has argued convincingly that it was the practice of Christians in praying to Christ as God that decisively influenced the course of the Arian controversy so that it ended with the acknowledgement of the full divinity of Christ:[25] "Whatever the intellectual merits of Dynamic Monarchianism, Origenist subordinationism, and philosophical Arianism, they failed very largely because they did not do justice to Christian apprehension of the Son as a fitting object of worship and adoration."[26] Pelikan agrees with this point of view. He suggests that Cyprian and Augustine were influenced in their doctrine of original sin by the practice of the Church of their day in baptizing infants.[27] And Wiles believes that it was the appeal by the Cappadocian Fathers to the use of the baptismal formula that played the largest part in winning acceptance for the doctrine of the divinity of the Holy Spirit.[28] Pelikan further argues that Athanasius was influenced by his Mariological doctrine, and not least in his use of the epithet *theotokos* for Mary, by the lives of ascetic virgins in Egypt, and by a local festival of Mary.[29]

Pelikan appears to think that the fact that Athanasius yielded to these influences was an advantage. He appears, further, to subscribe to the curious theory of what we might call "gods by grace." This was the idea, first mooted in Newman's *Development of Doctrine*, that the status which the Arians had envisaged for Christ and which was rejected for Christ by Nicene orthodoxy, could be, and was, suitably attributed to the Blessed Virgin Mary.[30] Several early Fathers, mainly Greek, had put forward the view that men in God's design are destined when they achieve everlasting glory to become gods; gods, that is, not by nature but by the grace of God.[31] This doctrine of divinization or apotheosis became a commonplace in Athanasius and the Cappadocian Fathers, it was accepted as orthodoxy in the Eastern Church, and today, especially after the work of Pseudo-Dionysius in the sixth century and Gregory Palamas in the fourteenth, is championed strongly by contemporary Eastern Orthodox theologians. Now, the Arians held that the Son was not God by nature or substance, but only because God willed him to be so, in other words the Arian Christ bore some resemblance to the orthodox man in glory. What has traditional Christian piety done for the Blessed Virgin Mary, in such dogmas as those of the Immaculate Conception and the Assumption, but to hold that she has anticipated this apotheosis by grace, so that she has been envisaged as holding much the same status as the Arians had envisaged for Christ? Can we say that theological congruity and popular devotion together have achieved a just and proper development of doctrine? Rahner in his recent *Foundations of the Christian Faith* has in effect revived this argument.[32]

I cannot assent to this hypothesis. My main reason is a rooted objection to the idea that man should in any sense or in any circumstances become a god or God. During the first three centuries the word *theos/deus* could be used to cover a large range of phenomena, from the sole and Almighty God of the Jews to an unimportant local godlet with much restricted powers, like Nodens at Lydney. But with the formation of the doctrine of the Trinity under the pressure of pro-Nicene doctrine in the fourth century this situation changed, and it used to be the glory and boast of the Catholic faith that it had changed. Gods and goddesses were now banished before the majesty of the one and only God Almighty, three Persons and one God, of Christian dogma. In the twentieth century when people refer to God they mean God Almighty and nobody less. Even when they swear profanely by God, it is the name of the Almighty and sole God which they misuse. Even those who deny God's existence do not even trouble to deny the existence of gods or goddesses, but of the one only monotheistic God. The word "God" has for a thousand years had no other meaning in European thought. The Nicene Creed has, so to speak, entered the bloodstream of European culture. To attach any other significance to the word "God" except this one is, strictly speaking, to produce a meaningless word. To revive, therefore, another sense of the word "God" applicable to men in their ultimate state or to the Blessed Virgin Mary in her present condition is not only undesirable, because it produces deep semantic confusion, but actually impossible because there is no generally accepted reality to which the word "God" in this use could correspond, nor any good reason for desiring to use the word "God" in any but its traditional sense.

We may therefore conclude that the attempt to rest the development of dogma on piety and theological congruity alone, without any support from Scripture and tradition, is an unsatisfactory enterprise liable to lead doctrine into some curious and by no means healthy positions. Wiles in his discussion of the influence of piety on the development of doctrine gives a warning similar to this,[33] and Rahner writes "we cannot—like the modernists—set up a wordless state of experience with regard to what is meant by faith to derive thence new and original statements of revelation in the form of intellectual assertions."[34] In short, though religious experience may—indeed must—contribute to doctrine, it cannot be a substitute for it.

This examination of the dogma of the Assumption of the Blessed Virgin Mary should lead us to conclude that it is highly unsatisfactory to emancipate the development of doctrine from all historical checks. The result is either a virtually uncontrolled doctrinal space flight in which one extravagant and outrageous development is piled upon another to build an apparently imposing structure on the flimsiest of foundations, or (what I suspect to be the Protestant reverse of the coin of which Catholic development is the obverse) a reduction of Christianity to a purely historical phenomenon like the development of Parliament whose evolution can move in whatever direction the whims of men dictate or the pressures of circumstances suggest. And when we speak about historical checks we realize at once that there can be only one primary check, Holy Scripture. I will therefore turn in the next chapter to making some suggestions about ways in which, even in the complex and confused theological situation of today, Scripture and development could and perhaps should interact.[35]

(6)

Contemporary Reassessment of Doctrine:

Models for Development

I

I first wish to make the point that the proper way of using Scripture is not to rely on one text or on a narrow basis of textual support in order to develop doctrine, as if any verse is as authoritative as any other, as if "the Word became flesh" is no more authoritative than "take a little wine for thy stomach's sake." Not only must we look for a wide basis of support in Scripture for any development, but we must recognize that some parts of the Bible are more authoritative than other parts. The Synoptic gospels are more authoritative than Judges, Romans more than Esther. And within the New Testament Romans is more authoritative than Jude, Hebrews than 3 John. This principle does not set up a canon within the canon, for it does not reject one part of the New Testament in favor of another, but tries to achieve a proper balance and proportion of the parts. Thus the fact that most of the documents of the New Testament speak of our sharing of the *life* of God or of Christ is not seriously impaired by the fact that 2 Peter speaks of us becoming sharers of the divine *nature*. It would be quite wrong to begin developing a doctrine of the destined apotheosis of man relying on this text alone.

The same principle can be applied more drastically to a more important doctrine. In the development of the doctrine of the Incarnation, and of the Mariological doctrines which are a development of this development, it has long been the practice, so much so as virtually to amount to what might be called Catholic tradition, to use as primary evidence the story of the Virginal Conception of Jesus—what is for short called the Virgin Birth. Putting aside the historical question of whether the Virgin Birth happened or not, a consideration of the amount of space devoted to it in the New Testament and the value attached to it in the thought of the New Testament must give the theologian pause. Two of the Synoptic evangelists record it among their Infancy Narratives and these are the two who also give genealogies of Jesus, genealogies which (in spite of the *hos enomizeto* of Luke 3:23) depend for their significance on Jesus being the son of Joseph! No other writer in the New Testament mentions the Virgin Birth, not Paul, not John, not the author of Hebrews. Either these writers did not know of it or, if they were aware of it, they did not think it important in their interpretation of the significance of Jesus Christ. Yet this report of the Virgin Birth ever since the time of Justin Martyr has been made the key factor in the development of the doctrine of the Incarnation and of Mariological dogma. The Council of Ephesus of 431 described Mary as ever-virgin, though no historical evidence to this effect could possibly have been available to it. Ambrose at the end of the fourth century first advances the argument that Christ's sinlessness should be connected with the Virgin Birth and the converse of this proposition that people not born of a virginal conception are inevitably sinful, and Augustine follows this hint eagerly in articulating his doctrine of inherited original sin.[1] Fourteen centuries later Newman can throw off the statement that matter was not originally evil but that it had been rendered corrupt by the Fall and that therefore the bit of matter which God took to himself (the body of Jesus) had first to be purified, by causing Mary to be immaculately conceived and Jesus to be born of a virginal conception.[2] How astounding and fantastic a development from an account in Scripture whose attestation is both ambiguous and sparse! If the development of doctrine is to correspond to the proportion of its attestation in Scripture, this is an utterly extravagant and irresponsible development.

II

Let us now look at another point which is perhaps even nearer to the heart of Christianity than the last. The early Christian Church assumed complacently that the Jewish nation had no further part to play in history, or, to put it another way, that God had rejected them from his divine plan. The Church had some apparently strong evidence on its side in making this assumption. With the Fall of Jerusalem in A.D. 70 the Jewish national state had been destroyed, the unity of the Jewish tradition was apparently lost, and the whole sacrificial cult in the Temple demolished for ever. Part of the explanation of the odious way in which Christians treated Jews during the Middle Ages arose from the Christians' belief that the Jews were an historical anachronism and one that upset the plans and purpose of God. They could have said what, according to Tertullian, the pagans used to say to the Christians of his day, *Non licet esse vos.* But we who live nearly two thousand years after the Fall of Jerusalem must surely wake up to the fact that the Jews are not going to disappear from history. In spite of the vilest and most thorough attempt to eliminate them by mass murder made in the history of the human race, on the part of the Nazis of Germany during the last World War, it is obvious that Jewry has survived, is in many respects flourishing, shows no sign of disappearing, and has indeed set up for itself a national state in Palestine, established by means of ruthless terrorist tactics, surviving by a savagely punitive policy, and enjoying the highest cost of living in the world, but still *there*.

The attitude of the writers of the New Testament to the Jews varies, reflecting a deepening hostility in proportion to the lateness of the documents. The Gospel according to St. Matthew can put into the mouths of the Jews at the trial of Christ the no doubt totally fictitious cry "His blood be on us and our children!"

(27:25). But set against this is the attitude of St. Paul, who as far as we can see never despaired of the possibility of the Jews finally accepting Jesus as the Christ, and the words of Jesus himself who not only teaches unconditional forgiveness of enemies but also never remotely hints that the Jews are outside the providence of God. Christians must adjust themselves to the perhaps unwelcome fact that the Jews as a nation, or separately indentifiable community with its own self-consciousness, serve a purpose in the providence of God and Christian doctrine must accommodate itself to this fact. Perhaps one way of advance here would be to return to the categories of thought of the Christians of the first and second centuries, and to develop them so as to be relevant to contemporary Jewish thought about God.

Another point which reaches far into the basic beliefs of Christianity is the fulfillment of prophecy. One of the strongest points in the preaching and teaching of the early Church was the claim that Jesus Christ fulfilled the prophecies of the Old Testament, and this conviction is to be found firmly embedded in the New Testament also. Now I believe that in a genuine and profound way this is true, that Jesus Christ is, as Paul puts it, the Amen to the promises of God and the fulfillment of many hopes and desires expressed in the Old Testament, but it is impossible any longer to believe that he is so in many, indeed most, of the ways which the writers of the New Testament and of the early Church imagined that he was. He did not fulfill in precise detail precisely detailed predictions about almost every incident of his career made by prophets hundreds of years before he was born. The concept of prediction must be radically revised and the concept of inspiration dropped altogether. This means a serious modification of much very ancient Christian tradition in the face of sheer fact and logic.

The subject of eschatology is also a relevant one here. At first sight, the eschatological element in the New Testament at least seems wholly obsolete and irrelevant. The Second Coming did not take place when it was ardently expected during the first Christian generation. Would it not have been better to remove eschatological concepts and language altogether from Christianity thenceforward? So thought Origen in the third century and many liberal Protestants in the nineteenth and twentieth. If that had been done we would have been spared much futile rousing of apocalyptic expectation during the course of Christian history, and avoided a neurosis which has afflicted the Christian soul too often and too long. But the Church did not completely abandon eschatology, any more than the author of the Fourth Gospel did. The Fourth Evangelist sublimated eschatology and in this sublimated form it has had a continuous influence on Christian doctrine and proved itself an indispensable, albeit bizarre and uncomfortable, element in Christianity. On the one hand it has ensured the ultimacy of the Christian claims for the significance of Christ; this man is so important that the only really important thing that can happen after his appearance is the end of the world. On the other hand it has ensured the discontinuity of God's activity in the scheme of salvation, the sense of Christ as an irruption, a new start. It is their utter neglect of eschatology that renders the recent work on Christian doctrine of such authors as John Hick, Maurice Wiles, and Geoffrey Lampe so implausible to the serious student of the Christian tradition.

I could mention other less important but still interesting points: the realization of the limits of Scripture, that, for instance, it gives us no information about a single authoritative form for the ministry and only very sparse information about the significance of the eucharist, which explains why the reformers of the sixteenth century could agree on their doctrine of grace and justification but could not agree on the ministry and the eucharist. Or I could refer to the controversy about the Filioque clause, which has been caused largely because of a wooden and narrow interpretation of some verses in the Fourth Gospel instead of an attempt to see the doctrine of the Holy Spirit in the context of the whole New Testament. But perhaps enough has been said to enable us to reach some conclusions about the vexed question of criteria for the development of doctrine. It is not necessary to abandon criteria for the development of doctrine; we are not called to jettison Scripture as an historical check on this development; on the contrary, it is vital to retain it, and to retain it as a norm and not simply as a base. Piety must be allowed as one element in the formation and the development of doctrine, but piety alone, accompanied only by that deceitful will-o'-the-wisp, theological congruity, is not an adequate criterion, indeed becomes a dangerous temptation.

Scripture can and must be used as a norm, but used with flexibility and breadth of understanding, and we must not flinch from some of the more disturbing consequences which flow from these principles, such as the placing of the Virgin Birth in an inconspicuous and peripheral position when we develop doctrine about the Incarnation. Tradition must indeed remain as a criterion. We cannot start Christianity again from a *tabula rasa,* nor from the Bible alone, nor wholly and consistently from any past point in history, be it the reformation of Martin Luther or the reformation of Martin Werner; we cannot ignore or abolish or undo the effect of continuity. But we must be prepared to reexamine and reassess tradition. Those options which apparently were closed centuries ago, such as the rejection of the Jews, and the predictory role of the Old Testament prophets, and almost all denominational conclusions about the form of the ministry, are in fact open and available for inspection again in the light of new knowledge and new insight. We must remember Wiles' criterion of creativity. Development appears to close options, but history has a way of opening them again. I do not mean that we can return with archaistic fervor to earlier doctrinal positions and mentalities. History never exactly repeats itself and it is impossible to turn its clock back. But development need not take place in the straight line of an ever-expanding, ever-increasing growth and articulation of a vast, unending system of doctrinal elaboration and speculation. It should have and will have its periods of reduction, retrenchment, reformation, and reconsideration as the anchor-line of Scripture pulls back the adventurous ship of development, or as the currents of secular thought to which the development of doctrine must always be sensitive set in different directions and alter course and temperature.

III

These nautical metaphors bring us suitably to the main point in this chapter, to the subject of models of development. We allow that development has certainly taken place and that there are norms and criteria for this development, albeit very flexible norms and criteria, themselves subject to certain possibilities of change. But further light may be thrown on the subject if we ask what pattern or analogy we can envisage to explain this development or make it coherent. If we are not to envisage development as totally unpredictable and uncontrolled, we ought to be able to point to some analogy or principle which might enable us to understand its course. Luther's position was that if a doctrine, however apparently inconsistent with the rest of Christian doctrine, was in Scripture, it must be believed, and if it was not in Scripture, it must be rejected, and that logical sequence has got nothing to do with developing doctrine.[3]

This is impossible; we cannot rule out logical sequence as a proper criterion for the development of doctrine. But in fact it is clear that logical sequence alone will not cover some of the causes of development which we have allowed as justified. And to invoke, as Newman invoked, the analogy of biological growth will not be sufficient either. There are too many discontinuities, reversals, and reductions in the history of doctrine for this to be a useful analogy. Wiles, in his *Remaking of Christian Doctrine*, rejects the appeal to logical analysis and the biological analogy as insufficient and reverts to one which he had suggested in his earlier *Making of Christian Doctrine*. This is the analogy of "other examples of development in the history of human thought," such as science or history.[4] "It is a new frame of reference rather than new particular facts ... which is most productive of advance," he says in the later book. The element of identity here lies in "a continuing similarity of shape or character which is compatible with some change in every particular." A little later he redefines such development as "change through alteration of perspective."[5] Rahner produces a particularly striking analogy, the analogy of a lover. He knows the object of his love deeply, densely, richly, without stating it in propositions fully or even adequately, and he also reflects upon it and can understand more about it and articulate that knowledge in propositions by reflecting upon it. He describes his idea thus:

> Original, non-propositional, unreflexive yet conscious possession

of a reality on the one hand, and reflexive (propositional), articulated consciousness of this original consciousness on the other—
these are not competing opposites but reciprocally inter-acting
factors of a single experience necessarily unfolding in historical
succession.[6]

He then enlarges upon this account of the original reception of
revelation and its unfolding in development thus:

> The objective connection between the new proposition and the
> old knowledge is not merely that between something logically
> explicit and something logically implicit in two propositions; it is
> rather a connection between what becomes partially explicit in a
> proposition and the unreflexive, total spiritual possession of the
> entire *res,* so that the explicit proposition is at the same time more
> and less than its implicit source.[7]

And he reminds his readers of the difference between what is
stated and what is communicated. A normal human proposition
cannot be exhaustively stated. There is in it "an intrinsic and
irreducible indistinctness of content." The proposition is a kind
of window opened to give a view of a thing, not "a package with
sharply defined contents."[8]

Pelikan sees development running on a principle of
"correction-and-fulfillment," instanced first in the taking over
by the Church of the heritage of Judaism, and later by such
examples as Athanasius seeking to justify his predecessors in
Trinitarian thought, Augustine attempting to show that his predecessors were not Pelagian in their doctrine, the orthodox opponents of Gottschalk in the ninth century seeking to justify
Augustine, the arguments between the Greek East and Latin
West which turned upon "the testimony of tradition," and the
determination of the Protestant reformers of the sixteenth century to demonstrate their loyalty to the Catholic tradition in spite
of Rome.[9]

Nicholas Lash has suggested yet another principle of continuity: this is a synthesis of Scripture, tradition, and the magis-
terium of the Church achieved as a kind of "recollection"
(*anamnesis*) in the liturgy: "it is the Church's task in every age to
seek so to relate to its past . . . as to enable that past, interpreted

in the present, effectively to function as a challenge: a challenge to look and think and trust, and act in the direction of that future which is promised to us in the New Testament."[10]

All these analogies and observations are useful and together suggest that development can be seen as a coherent and ultimately reasonable process. In particular the analogy from the progress of some humane study, such as Shakespearean criticism, seems to me valuable. Here change, vicissitude, reversal, radical critique, the appearance of new viewpoints and approaches, the constant influence of the changing pattern of secular thought, all play their part in a unity of study and subject which certainly does not proceed in a simple line of ever-increasing insight and unanimity, but does in the long run gradually contribute to an increased understanding of Shakespeare's works, which the actual performance of his plays enhances considerably. We have only to consider the very different treatment of Shakespeare's work during the seventeenth century, during the eighteenth century, in the nineteenth century, and in our own century to appreciate this point. The young Milton could write patronizingly of hearing

> Sweetest Shakespeare, Fancy's child
> Warble his native woodnotes wild.

The eighteenth century appreciated Shakespeare (witness Garrick's festival at Stratford-on-Avon), but it could also commit the egregious solecism of adding a happy ending to King Lear. The nineteenth century bowdlerized and sentimentalized Shakespeare. Our own age has returned to a fuller and more detailed investigation of Shakespeare's work, acting his plays, inter alia, in the costume of a dozen different ages, but it has also, quite recently, rivalled the bad taste of the eighteenth century by producing *Measure for Measure* with an unhappy, or at least a squalid, ending. In a sense every age judges itself by its reaction to Shakespeare. And yet we can never say that we know more about Shakespeare's works than he did himself. He wrote them. They came out of his living experiences as they do not out of ours. Revelation, so to speak, cannot be repeated, but prayer and worship (i.e., the acting of the plays) can constantly return to it.

Pelikan's principle of "correction-and-fulfilment," however, seems to me to be the nearest to the mark. Indeed, we have on more than one occasion in the course of this book found the expression "trial and error" the most appropriate one to use to describe the development of doctrine, and the last proposition put forward in this chapter will be that the most honest and satisfactory account of the development of doctrine is to say that it has been conducted upon a principle of trial and error. Not only is this manifestly the way in which other parallel disciplines have proceeded, but we have seen plenty of examples in the course of our survey of the continuity of Christian doctrine to suggest that experiment, and the necessary concomitant of experiment, error, has played a large part in this process, and that it would be totally wrong and dishonest to say that the error was only on the part of the heretics and the correction on the part of the orthodox. The best and wisest of theologians have fallen into some error, and sometimes what was thought of as established orthodoxy in one age has been branded heresy by a later age. The matter has been admirably put by George Tyrrell:

> For him [that is, the Modernist], however, it is a double process of good and evil; of false and true. He recognizes, what the reformers could not recognize with their dim historical light, that the tares were sown almost contemporaneously with the wheat; and are always being sown; that if the wheat has grown the tares have also grown even from the Apostolic age—from the first pious tamperings with the Gospel text; that there has been a development not only of good but of evil principles, not only of truths but of errors, not only of the leaven of the Gospel but of the leaven of hypocrisy. He sees that in every generation some tare or another ripens and betrays its true character and needs to be uprooted; that there are epochs when a perfect harvest of such tares demands a sort of revolution—a ruthless thrusting in of the sickle of criticism, a binding in bundles and burning of noxious weeds.[11]

Rahner (who cannot, of course, admit error in development) says with praiseworthy honesty that it is better to describe development as a process of becoming conscious of dogma than to say that the Church now believes what it did not believe in the past.[12] But our survey of development has at least enabled us to realize that the Church has in the past believed what it does not now believe, that it has achieved consciousness of dogma by a process of experiment which has not excluded error on the part both of these who are styled orthodox and Catholic and of those who are styled heretical and non-Catholic.

Perhaps we can invoke as a guide here what Pelikan has said about the unity of the Church. The empirical unity of the Church, he suggests, should be for us what the empirical holiness of the Church was for Augustine, "a process and a goal rather than a prior fact." And he adds, "both the unity of the Church and its holiness would then be seen as perfect gifts to the Church, but at the same time as goals for the Church's life and growth." We can apply this to the truth with which the Church has been intrusted. It is a truth which the Church has not invented, a truth which apprehends the Church and gives it life, but which it has to apprehend slowly and painfully, by a rigorous process of trial and error, and if we are to understand properly the continuity of Christian doctrine we are driven to seek for a properly flexible and comprehensive concept of the Church. The last word will lie with Pelikan:

> As the study of historical theology compels one to ask how such a variety of doctrines could have developed within the Christian community, so a truly Catholic ecclesiology enables one to come to terms with this variety.[13]

The subject of the development of doctrine leads us inexorably to the subject of ecclesiology. The theologians of the ecumenical world are called to consider more seriously than ever before the nature, responsibility, and functioning of the Church in the world today.

References

Chapter 1
1. Dennis Nineham, *The Use and Abuse of the Bible* (London, 1976).
2. J.H. Plumb, *The Death of the Past* (London, 1969), p. 17.
3. Ibid., p. 105.
4. Ibid., p. 106.
5. Ibid., pp. 136–142, quotation from p. 142.
6. Van A. Harvey, *The Historian and the Believer* (London, 1965).
7. Hans-Georg Gadamer, *Truth and Method* (English translation, 1975, of original German edition, Tübingen, 1960), p. 108.
8. Truesdell S. Brown, *The Greek Historians* (Lexington, Mass., 1973).
9. Ibid., p. 152.
10. Herodotus, *Histories* II.86–88.
11. Herodotus, *Histories* III.26.
12. Herodotus, *Histories* IV.135–139.
13. Brown, *Greek Historians,* p. 133, n. 40.
14. Ibid., pp. 157, 158.
15. Gerald Downing, "Our Access to Other Cultures, Past and Present," *The Modern Churchman*, vol. 21, no. 1 (Winter 1977), pp. 28–42.
16. Harvey, *Historian*, p. 283
17. David Pailin, "Lessing's Ditch Revisited," in *Theology and Change,* ed. R.H. Preston (London, 1975), pp. 78–103.
18. Harvey, *Historian*, p. 284.
19. I do not deal here with Dr. Pailin's appeal to the impossibility of achieving a correct perspective for appreciating events from a study of events put forward in his essay in *Theology and Change*. Perhaps what is said in the next section will sufficiently indicate that nobody ever does attempt to achieve such a correct perspective for appreciating events from a study of the events *alone*, but that this does not preclude the possibility of understanding history, and therefore, of course, of history's providing a motive for faith.
20. Harvey, *Historian*, p. 283.
21. Gadamer, *Truth and Method*, p. 410.

22. Ibid., p. 310 *et alibi*; cf. Nicholas Lash, *Change in Focus* (London, 1973), pp. 168–175.
23. Gadamer, *Truth and Method*, p. 324.

Chapter 2

1. See Jaroslav Pelikan, *Historical Theology: Continuity and Change in Christian Doctrine* (Chicago and New Haven, 1971), pp. 33–67.
2. London 1878, the republication of an article in the *Christian Remembrancer* of January 1847. References to Newman's *Development* are to the edition of 1845 (not the revised edition of 1878), recently reissued as a Pelican Classic (Harmondsworth, 1973), with an introduction by J.M. Cameron.
3. E.g., cap. III, sec. iii, 198–199; sec iv. 209; cap. VIII, sec. v,, 398–399.
4. E.g., cap. VI, sec, i, 337 n, the whole revelation not contained in Scripture; cap. VIII, sec. i, 418, "the mind of the Church working out dogmatic truths from implicit feelings under supernatural guidance." Mozley comments upon this ambiguity, *Theory of Development*, pp. 198–200.
5. Mozley, ibid., p. 33.
6. Ibid., p. 40.
7. Ibid., pp. 133–134.
8. Ibid., pp. 198–200.
9. Ibid., p. 206.
10. Ibid., pp. 150–209; cf. especially the naïve statement: "If, in short, a doctrine of inspiration means, as everybody supposes it to mean, a doctrine of which the Apostles were informed by inspiration, and, being informed of, taught, the Lord's Divinity is, upon the theory we are dealing with, not a doctrine of inspiration" (p. 209).
11. Nicholas Lash, *Newman on Development* (London, 1975), p. 17.
12. Ibid., p. 75.
13. And also with Karl Rahner, if we are to follow his essays on development (to which reference will be made later).
14. Newman, *Development*, cap. III, sec. iii, pp. 198–199 (quotation from 199).
15. Lash, *Change in Focus*, pp. 119–127.
16. Mozley recognized and criticized this principle of "whatever is, is right," *Theory*, pp. 117, 118.
17. Lash, *Change in Focus*, pp. 119–127.
18. Ibid., pp. 134–136.
19. Ibid., p. 145.
20. Ibid., p. 147.
21. The process has been usefully set out by Harald Wagner, *An den Ursprüngen des frühkatholischen Problems: Die Ortsbestimmung des Katholizismus in älteren Luthertum* (Frankfurt, 1973).

22. As I did in *The Bible as a Norm of Faith* (University of Durham, 1963), p. 3.

23. Lash, *Change in Focus*, pp. 1–12.

24.. London, 1974: because this is a small book dealing with a large subject and because of the tentativeness of the author's treatment of it, it is best to regard the whole book as a proof of this statement; one could refer particularly to pp. 2–4, where two American authors are quoted as saying that in his earlier work, *The Making of Christian Doctrine*, Wiles had in effect abandoned the idea of the development of doctrine in favor of a "continuing activity theory"; or one could refer to pp. 29–31, where Wiles argues that it is virtually impossible in present circumstances to construct a "closely articulated structure of beliefs" (p. 34) about God. But it is better to appeal to the book as a whole. We shall return to this point later.

25. See above, pp. 3–4.

26. D. A Pailin, "Authenticity in the Interpretation of Christianity," in *The Cardinal Meaning* (Mouton Publishers: The Hague and Paris, 1978, Religion and Reason Series 6), pp. 127–155.

27. Hans Küng, *On Being a Christian* (New York, 1976), p. 461. He devotes less than six pages to Mary in a book of 606 pages.

28. Ibid., 461–462.

29. Karl Rahner, "Considerations on the Development of Dogma," in *Theological Investigations* IV (E. T. Baltimore and London, 1966), p. 17.

30. Rahner, "The Development of Dogma," in *Theological Investigations* I (E. T. Baltimore and London, 1961), pp. 73–75.

31. Rahner, *Foundations of the Christian Faith* (New York, 1978), pp. 387, 388.

32. Lash, *Change in Focus*, p. 163.

33. Ibid., pp. 59–72 and 175–176, the quotation from the latter passage.

34. Pailin, "Authenticity," pp. 156–159. Admittedly, his argument is incomplete and he hopes to complete it in a later article.

35. *Panta konis kai panta gelōs kai panta to mēden. Panta gar ex alogón esti ta gīnomena.*

Chapter 3

1. 1 Cor. 16:23; *Didache X.6*.

2. Ignatius, *Magnesians* 8:2.

3. Origen, *Philocalia* (ed. J.A. Robinson) XV. 12, *Contra Celsum* VI.75.

4. Jaroslav Pelikan, *Development of Christian Doctrine* (New Haven and London, 1969), pp. 13–14; himself a Lutheran, he has noticed this tendency among what he calls Protestants.

5. Harvey, *Historian*, p. 282.

6. Pelikan, *The Christian Tradition*, Vol. I, *The Emergence of the Catholic Tradition (100–600)* (Chicago and London, 1971-), p. 70.
7. Harvey, *Historian*, p. 284.
8. Wolfhart Pannenberg "Dogmatic Theses on the Doctrine of Revelation," in *Revelation as History*, ed. Pannenberg (New York, 1968), p. 151.

Chapter 4
1. Eusebius, *Adversus Marcellum* (Klostermann, rev. Hansen 1972 of 1906, GCS ser.) I.1.8 (PG 24.728.)
2. Gregory of Nazianzus, *Orationes* XXIII (VI) Migne (*PG* 35:I), pp. 1157, 1160; Gregory Nyssa, *Contra Eunomium* (ed. Jaeger) III (II) pp. 120–122.
3. E.g. Gregory Nyssa, *Contra Eunomium* (Jaeger) III (VI), pp. 35–39, *Refutatio Conf. Eunomii* (Jaeger), pp. 91–96; Gregory of Nazianzus, *Theol. Orat.* (Mason) V, pp. 31, 32, 33; *Poemata Dogmatica* 3.61–69 (Migne *PG* 37.1.413).
4. Wiles, *The Making of Christian Doctrine*, p. 100.
5. Ibid., pp. 129–130, E.P. Meijering, *Orthodoxy and Platonism in Athanasius* (Leiden, 1968). See also Pelikan, *Catholic Tradition*, pp. 210–220.
6. Meijering, *Orthodoxy and Platonism*, pp. 10–40, 88–90, 129–131.
7. "To Athanasius, Platonic ontology is not a purpose in itself, but a tool, which he is constantly using," Meijering, ibid., p. 131.
8. Wiles, *The Making of Christian Doctrine*, pp. 131–157, and especially 139–140.
9. Ibid., pp. 134–135.
10. Ibid., p. 137.
11. Ibid., pp. 138–139, 157.
12. R.P.C. Hanson, "Dogma and Formula in the Fathers," *Studia Patristica* 13, ii (1975), pp. 169–184.
13. Pelikan, *Catholic Tradition*, p. 223.
14. Basil, *De Spiritu Sancto* (Pruche 1946) xxii.53(*PG*32.168); *Adv. Eunom.* 1.17 (*PG* 29.552); 2.8 (*PG* 29.585); 24.1 (*PG* 29.628); *Epistles* (Courtonne) XXXVIII.4.19–22; CXXXIV (Deferrari) 1.2; (CCXXXV (Deferrari)) 1–3; Gregory Naz., *Theol. Orat.* ((Mason) II.5; XXIII.xi (*PG* 35.1164); Gregory of Nyssa, *Contra Eunom* (Jaeger) I.498; II.13, 93–102; III.(i)108,(viii) 7–12; *Refut. Conf. Eunom.* (Jaeger) 17; *Catechet. Discourse* (Meridier) XV.1.
15. Meijering, *Orthodoxy and Platonism*, p. 188.
16. Pannenberg, *Revelation as History*, pp. 135–136; see also p. 16.
17. Harnack, *Dogmengeschichte* I (1931) 20, as quoted by Pelikan, *Catholic Tradition*, p. 55.
18. Pelikan, *Catholic Traditon*, p. 70.
19. Meijering, *God Being History*, pp. 9–11.

20. See Pannenberg, *Basic Questions in Theology*, II (London and Philadelphia, 1970-[E.T. of 1967 German ed.]), pp. 9-11, 136-40; Meijering, *God Being History*, p. 18.
21. E.g., Pelikan, *Historical Theology*, p. 76; R. Murray, *Symbols of the Kingdom* (Cambridge, 1975).

Chapter 5
1. Pelikan, *Development*, pp. 23-24.
2. Ibid., p. 51; the references to Harnack are from the fifth German ed. (Tübingen, 1931) I, pp. 21-22, and III, pp. 861-863.
3. Pelikan, *Historical Theology*, p. 79.
4. Pelikan, *Development*, pp. 16-18, quotation from p. 16.
5. But not quite: he seems to agree (pp. 2-4) with the critics of his earlier *Making of Christian Doctrine* who say that in effect he abandons the concept of the development of doctrine. But in fact (pp. 4-19) he does agree that there are one or two workable models for development. As he goes on, however, afterwards to abandon Christology or Incarnation or finally any theory that sees God active in one series of events rather than in them all, he leaves little material for speaking meaningfully about development.
6. See W.O. Chadwick's *From Bossuet to Newman* (Cambridge, 1957).
7. Pelikan, *Historical Theology*, p. 156.
8. Ibid., pp. 156-157, quotation from p. 157.
9. Ibid., pp. 157-161, quotations from p. 158.
10. Ibid., p. 158.
11. Ibid., p. 159.
12. Ibid., p. 160.
13. Cf. Pelikan's suggestion that the concentration of the Second Council of Constantinople in 553 upon anathematizing the Antiochene school and Origenism distracted the attention of theologians from the undesirable tendencies in the thought of Pseudo-Dionysius: "There is both historical significance and theological irony in the chronological coincidence between the condemnation of Origen and the rise of Dionysian mysticism, for most of the doctrines on account of which the Second Council of Constantinople anathematized Origen were far less dangerous to the tradition of Catholic orthodoxy than was the Crypto-Origenism canonized in the works of Dionysius the Areopagite" (*Catholic Tradition*, p. 348).
14. E.T. of original German (1957) London, 1964.
15. See, e.g., *Modern Eucharistic Agreement* (London, 1973) and *Modern Ecumenical Documents on the Ministry* (London, 1975).
16. Bernard Lonergan in *The Way to Nicaea* (London, 1976), a book which in other respects I find derivative and schematic, has some

useful remarks on pp. 136–7 about the Nicene dogma supporting this point of view.

17. Rahner, "The Development of Dogma," *Theological Investigations* I (39–77), p. 48. The exact date of the original publication of the essay in German is not given in the E. T., but it must have been some time before 1961. Nicholas Lash also refers to this point in *Change in Focus* (pp. 15, 16), though I do not think that he handles it as well as Rahner does.

18. Ibid., p. 49.

19. Rahner, "Consideration on the Development of Dogma," *Theological Investigations* IV (3–35) p. 9. This essay was first published in German in *Zeitschrift für Katholische Theologie* 80 (1958), pp. 1–16, but was originally composed and delivered as a paper for a congress of German professors of dogmatic theology at Innsbruck, 3rd October 1957.

20. Rahner, *Th. Investigations* I, p. 67.

21. Pelikan, *Development*, p. 112.

22. Wiles, *Making of Christian Doctrine*, pp. 170–171.

23. Ibid. pp. 171–173. Compare Lash's list of signs of continuity, given earlier, pp. 39–40.

24. Wiles, *Remaking of Christian Doctrine*, pp. 2–4.

25. Wiles, *Making of Christian Doctrine*, pp. 56–70.

26. Ibid., p. 87.

27. Pelikan, *Development*, pp. 73–94.

28. Wiles, *Making of Christian Doctrine*, 80ff. Neither he nor Pelikan appears to have observed that the first theologian to make appeal to the practice of baptism in theological argument is neither Basil in *De Spiritu Sancto* nor Athanasius (who does use this appeal in *Letters to Sarapion*), but Eusebius of Caesarea, *Adversus Marcellum* (ed. E. Klostermann, GCS ser. 1906, rev. Hansen 1972) I.1.8.

29. Pelikan, *Development*, pp. 95–119.

30. Newman, *Development of Doctrine*, Cap. VII, Sec. I, pp. 402–411; Mozley demolished this theory, *Theory of Development*, pp. 52–81; Wiles refers to it without enthusiasm, *Making of Christian Doctrine*, p. 107. Pelikan treats of it in *Development*, pp. 116–119, 144.

31. E.g., Clement of Alexandria, *Protrepticus* 1.8.4 (GCS ser.); Origen, *De Oratione* 27:13 (GCS ser.); *Contra Celsum* 3.28 (GCS ser.); see Pelikan, *Catholic Tradition*, p. 155.

32. Rahner, *Foundations of Christian Faith*, pp. 387, 388.

33. *Making of Christian Doctrine*, pp. 88–90.

34. Rahner, *Theological Investigations* IV, 13.

35. Others, of course, have made similar suggestions: Wiles, *The Making of Christian Doctrine*, pp. 174–180; Pelikan, *Development*, pp. 67–69.

Chapter 6
1. Pelikan, *Catholic Tradition*, pp. 290–291.

2. Newman, *Development of Doctrine,* cap. VIII, sec. 1, p. 378.
3. Pelikan, *Development,* p. 66.
4. Wiles, *Making of Christian Doctrine,* pp. 169ff., *Remaking of Christian Doctrine,* pp. 4–9. As Lash points out (*Change in Focus,* p. 110), Newman and Loisy had already suggested the model of literary criticism. See further below, pp. 124–126.
5. Wiles, *Remaking,* p. 7. I omit his further analogy, of the shape of the human face remaining the same through growth and change, because it is only Newman's biological analogy in another form.
6. Rahner, *Th. Investigations* I, pp. 64–67; quotation from p. 65.
7. Ibid., p. 67.
8. Ibid., p. 68–73, quotations from p. 69.
9. Pelikan, *Catholic Tradition,* p. 15.
10. Lash, *Change in Focus,* p. 72.
11. Tyrrell, *Mediaevalism* (London 1909), p. 149.
12. Rahner, *Th. Investigations* IV.
13. Pelikan, *Historical Theology,* p. 160.

Suggestions for Further Reading

Barr, James *The Bible in the Modern World*. London: SCM Press, 1973.
_____, *Explorations in Theology: The Scope and Authority of the Bible*. London: SCM Press, 1980.
Biemer, G., *Newman On Tradition*. Translated and edited by Kevin Smith. Rev. ed. Freiburg: Herder; London: Burns & Oates, 1967.
Bruce, F.F., *Tradition: Old and New*. Exeter: Paternoster Press, 1970.
Campenhausen, H. von, *Tradition and Life in the Church*. London: Collins Publishers, 1968.
Chirico, Peter, *Infallibility: The Crossroads of Doctrine*. Mission, Kansas: Sheed Andrews and McMeel, 1977.
Congar, Yves, *Tradition and Traditions*. London: Burns & Oates, 1966.
Coulson, John, *Newman and the Common Tradition: A Study in Language of Church and Society*. New York: Oxford University Press, 1970.
Dyson, Anthony O., *The Immortality of the Past*. London: SCM Press, 1974.
Florovsky, Georges, *Bible, Church, Tradition: An Eastern Orthodox View*. Belmont, Mass.: Nordland Publishing Co., 1972.
Geiselmann, J.R., *The Meaning of Tradition*. Translated from the German by W.J. O'Hara. London: Burns & Oates, 1966.
Hanson, R.P.C., *Tradition in the Early Church*. London: SCM Press, 1962.
Lash, Nicholas, *Voices of Authority*. Shepherdstown, W. Va.: Patmos Press, 1976.
Mackey, J.P., *The Modern Theology of Tradition*. London: Darton, Longman & Todd, 1965.
_____, *Tradition and Change in the Church*. Dublin: Gill & Macmillan, 1968.
Newman, J.H., *An Essay in Aid of a Grammar of Assent*. Notre Dame, Indiana: University of Notre Dame Press, 1979. (London, 1870).
Richardson, Alan, *History Sacred and Profane*. London: SCM Press, 1964.
Schneidan, H.N., *Sacred Discontent: The Bible and Western Tradition*. Baton Rouge, La.: Louisiana State University Press, 1976.
Seynaeve, Jaak, *Cardinal Newman's Doctrine on Holy Scripture*. Louvain: Publications Universitaires de Louvain, 1953.

Tavard, George H., *Holy Writ or Holy Church*. London: Burns & Oates, 1959.

Thisleton, A.C., *The Two Horizons*. Exeter: Paternoster Press, 1980.

Todd, J.M., ed., *Problems of Authority: Fourth Downside Symposium*. London: Darton, Longman & Todd, 1962.

Walgrave, J.H., *Newman the Theologian*. Translated by A.V. Littledale. New York: Sheed and Ward, 1960.